Penguin Education
Penguin English Project Stage One

**Teachers' Handbook**

# Penguin English Project

# Stage One Teachers' Handbook

Penguin Books

Penguin Books Ltd, Harmondsworth,
Middlesex, England
Penguin Books Australia Ltd,
Ringwood, Victoria, Australia

First published 1972
Copyright © Patrick Radley and contributors, 1972

Made and printed in Great Britain by
W. Heffer and Sons Ltd, Cambridge

Set in IBM Press Roman

# Contents

# Introduction
## Patrick Radley

The first aim of Penguin English Project is to be of practical use to the teacher. But in the initial discussions to launch Stage One, we soon found that we were calling in question central ideas about English in school. The books bear the marks of these discussions; and, in what follows, four of their main characteristics are related to some of the most important theoretical issues.

### Open format

There are no instructions to either children or teachers in any of the six books in Stage One of PEP. These are books which leave us to find our own way about them. They are for discovery, for browsing through, for dipping into, for using in a relaxed way so that curiosity can take us at our own speed. If we are 'held' by a passage, that is because we have allowed it to make its own demands on us, not because we have been directed to it. Nor are there any indications of any 'use' to which the passages should be put. Their first 'use' is their existence and the response which any reader makes to them. That this response may give rise to subsequent activity is important, but not primarily so.

In the English classroom we set up an artificial situation so that certain things can happen. The most important of these is just 'being'. Only if we can let the children 'be', shall we have created an atmosphere in which they have scope to find themselves and to respond fully to the world around them. This is no invitation to disorder; tyranny of any kind, by teacher or children, is going to cause distracting and irrelevant tensions. It is a plea for the making of classroom relationships from which there can arise the order based on mutual knowledge and respect. In this atmosphere 'being' may take the form of just responding wholeheartedly to what is communicated in passage or picture. For some, perhaps many, of the children an ordered classroom may be the only place where they make this kind of full reaction, free of outside stultifying and distorting pressures.

Providing a chance for relaxed involvement has not been traditionally the role of the teacher. Too many of us struggle still to test our powers of instruction by devising exercises for the children which we can measure or grade; and in this we are amply assisted by the country's examination system. But it is not possible to mark the Inner Light, and 'becoming oneself' is not a competitive process. How can children respond fully to this or that passage in a climate of tests and competition? Since some will be less affected than others by these, there will be children whose confidence will wane at the expense of others'. And this precious quality, confidence, without which none of us ever achieve anything of real value, will be sapped by the system which we so painstakingly apply.

Nevertheless, in the English classroom we have, among other things, to encourage skills; and our patience and cunning is going to be sufficiently tested if we are to do this within the terms set out above. Ways whereby PEP Stage One Books may be used with these aims in mind come naturally under the headings which are to follow.

## Quality of material

An attempt has been made to put only good material into these books, to pick each passage or picture as being the best of its kind that could be found. The criterion has always included attractiveness, relevance and intrinsic interest. If children are to become involved there needs to be some powerful incentive that makes them want to look further and away from the immediate shifting world. But they, as we, have little respect for the gimmick; and only a feeling that what they are looking at or reading is relevant to them and of real interest will hold their attention once the first impact has gone.

We have too often assumed that children will swallow anything in school provided they can be persuaded of its ultimate tenuous connection with some final aim, the passing of an examination or the acquiring of a job. Immediate relevance is sacrificed for the attainment of a marketable commodity; what we come to expect of children is on a narrow front of our own making and has little to do with the business of being eleven, twelve or thirteen. In devising their own forms of underground resistance to what is demanded of them, children naturally come to assume that school and life have little in common, an assumption that many of them are going to carry over into their attitudes to work after they leave.

If we can see the point of what we are doing, how patiently, for instance, we wade through the small print of the advertisement pages to find a bargain or acquire the jargon of a handbook in order to effect a lasting repair. In school, motivation can be as practical, but need not be; it can include the desire to know more, to solve and to interpret, to respond to emotion with emotion, to explore details. If the picture or passage satisfies, it will call out from us an effort of attention; the determination to understand meaning, the stretching of imagination to ally ourselves to what is said, the struggle to hold parts in relation to the whole. None of these skills is easy to acquire, but we all need all of these and others. Though their acquisition may not take the form of a measurable activity nor seem to be painful, yet hard work is taking place.

Much of what is in these books is chosen because it can extend experience and widen response. From the limited world of our own interests and desires we need to be prompted to make imaginative jumps whereby we can see the human relevance of other experiences, other situations; and from that moment a new dimension has been added to our lives. Here, too, we have come to expect minimal results from children, neglecting the wealth of quick emotional responses that can take them into deep involvement outside themselves. Humour, pity, fear, disgust, delight, astonishment, these and other emotions in varying degrees and mixtures will be aroused by these pages. The concrete poem, the joke, the riddle, the extract from a note-book, or the cartoon, may all take on for a moment the task which has been recognized to be supremely that of imaginative literature, working 'by imaginatively prompting suggestion, so that the reader sees and takes in immediate perception what logic, analysis and statement can't convey'.

## Range of material

There is no special way to read or look at any of the books in Stage One of PEP; we should all be able to suit ourselves. Traditionally the classroom has been a place where everyone does the same thing for much of the time, and a teacher is thought successful if he can make this happen. But children are so different from one another that we should be suspicious of any method that aims frequently at uniformity. The range of material in these books assumes a diversity of approach and reaction; we won't all like the same things, nor like them in the same ways. The sharing by a whole class of one experience can be very enjoyable and memorable; but it is only one kind of response. Between that and the absorbed individual's silent attention lie all sorts of possible experiences, shared by any number at any level.

These are only first reactions; others follow, and are as diverse and unpredictable. We may want, for example, to look more closely at meaning or implication, to communicate a similar feeling or idea, pursue a subject to find out more about it, or, reacting to form or pattern, to try to do likewise. None of these directions, nor any of other possible ones, demands a particular activity or a predetermined number of people. But in a situation where choices are being made, a solution will grow naturally, suiting the moment and the particular individuals. Certainly the extent of variety in the books assumes that their use will probably lead to a range of activities going on in the classroom, or in extensions of it, at one and the same time. There are sometimes considerable difficulties in catering for this, though these can be over-estimated to hide an unwillingness to change or organize. One solution, available where the timetable can be tailored to it, is team teaching; rooms, resources and teachers can be pooled during certain times across, say, one whole year-group. This allows for flexibility and for sharing of ideas and responsibility; many teachers would find a sense of simple relief in exchanging their lonely autonomy for a few periods to become one of a team.

For we need each other's ideas; one person's reserves are not enough since, within the school limitations (and even these walls are loosening!), in English 'anything goes'. One factor only unites all the varied activities we set up; though each must be of the quality that allows of full involvement, it can be said to be less important in itself than as a means to an end. Take poetry, for instance. We may encourage children to read and examine poems, to experiment with methods of saying them individually or in groups with or without a tape-recorder, or setting them to noises, music or pictures, miming or dramatizing them, to collect their own or others' into small anthologies, in hand-outs or on wall posters, to listen to them on the radio or from records, to write doggerel, concrete poems, haikus or narrative poems, poems of personal feeling or poems of a factual nature. But in doing all this we are not trying to turn out poets; they will happen despite us! We are allowing children to be true partners of the poet, with an entry through poetry into the widest possible world of human and timeless experience, to add new dimensions to their own terms of expression and their capacity for receiving what other people say.

In the final analysis, these new dimensions are both ends and means, in an interacting process of growth. For we learn by coming to terms with our experience, finding the right way of describing it, of communicating it to others; but in this very process a certain re-making of ourselves goes on, a 'becoming ourselves' in the effort of communication. The means (provision of experience) and the end (personal development) are not separable and any attempt to mechanize means in the belief that we can make short cuts to ends is bound to fail. Annie Sullivan, Helen Keller's teacher, wrote:

I never taught language for the purpose of teaching it, but invariably used language as a medium for the communication of thought . . . no amount of language training will enable our . . . children to use language with ease and fluency unless they have something clearly in their minds which they wish to communicate, or unless we succeed in awakening in them a desire to know what is in the minds of others.

Range and variety of material are provided in the books of Stage One PEP to help stimulate these central desires and to provide or provoke the stuff of experience in a classroom situation.

## Themes

Though our cunning and patience may be stretched in ensuring quality and devising variety, we need them also to help us introduce order into this freedom. At the outset the framing of experience in themes is a convenient method of bringing infinite possibilities into manageable classroom shape; and these books are centred round six aspects of life thought to be of particular appeal to the eleven to thirteen year old. Most children of this age are curious and uncomplicated; thoughtful beyond their earlier cheerful inquisitiveness but retaining their capacity for enjoyment, they lack the frequent brooding self-awareness of the fourteen to fifteen year old. The themes of these books were chosen with these characteristics in mind and are largely reality-based and outward-looking in attitude. Such generalizations are only clumsy guides, and any group of children and teachers will need to work out their own ways of approach alongside which these books can be used.

But arrangement of work around a theme is for the sake of convenience rather than as a principle of order. The basis of order is elsewhere, and should be explicit and implicit in all that we do in English. It lies in the relationship between thought and language, in growth of understanding, and in problems of communication. Its start is in saying what one wants to say, when one wants to say it. If we have fulfilled our role as teachers by creating contexts in which this can happen, it is likely that children will soon become aware of the struggle to make language right. No discipline that we can invent is as useful as the children's own developing awareness that they have not said what they want to say, or that they have not communicated to others; but the situation must be one in which they have the confidence to experiment and to be led to a realization of the things that can go wrong. In the classroom, therefore, all must be speakers and spoken-to, writers and readers of what the others have written, sharers in success and failure. While the general emphasis must be on communication happening, not on its failure to happen, the teacher's job is to encourage a gradual and proper growth of self-criticism against the background of a great deal of practice in a wealth of real contexts. Moreover, it is only in this connection that conceptions of what is good and bad English, of what is right and wrong speech, can have any meaning. Where communication breaks down, there language has been inadequate; but awareness of the kind of language suitable to the context is crucial. With growth in knowledge of the range and quality of language-situations should come increasing awareness of fitness. In the widest possible sense, fitness is all.

The development of certain technical skills has been the normal yard-stick for 'progress' in English. It is a proper one, but disastrously narrow. From what has been said above it will be clear that the Stages of PEP are related to one another on the basis of growth in understanding, and of the developing complexity of the things that children wish to communicate, to themselves, to each other and to others. If they are encouraged to talk and write about real things, about things they know to be close to their experience, they will come to know whether or not they are satisfying their own acute need to understand and communicate. As teachers we are no different from them in this respect; where we differ is in the exercise of our art to enable that development to take place, and this may include resisting demands that measurable attainments be substituted for genuine growth. And when we have provided suitable conditions, fed in relevant material, shown sympathy and applauded success, we must know, as final evidence of 'progress', when we are not needed.

In what follows the editors of the six books have been given a free hand to establish in an introduction the aims of their selection, and to say in the accompanying notes whatever they think may be helpful to the teacher. No attempt has been made to achieve any overall unity or to avoid overlapping of methods and ideas, in the belief that there should be as many different teaching styles as there are teachers. But readers of the handbook should be able to dip into it where they see kindred ideas, and go away with their own intuitions confirmed and encouraged.

# Creatures Moving
## Geoffrey Summerfield

### 'It Was Good' (Genesis, i, 21)

This collection is based on a recognition not of '*all* things bright and beautiful' but of the extraordinary variety of the natural world, both exotic and near at hand, of kids' unforced interest in this world and of the precariousness of the world. It is therefore, in part, tendentious, and aims not only to present a series of celebrations of the excellent variety of natural forms but also to create a proper sense of concern about man's squandering and abuse of natural life. Another recurrent strand is the affinity of man and creature — the sense of likeness within or beneath unlikeness, of transpositions of human and non-human life, and of sustaining and occasionally puzzling interactions between them.

### Work in English and real life

It's a great pity that at 11+ children leave behind what is often the very rich environment of the junior-school classroom, with its vivarium, aquarium* and plants, to enter the verbalizing world of the secondary school.

We must ensure that, at this point, our pupils continue to have something worthwhile to verbalize, to record, to make observations on, to celebrate; and one of the best ways of doing this is to recognize, to admit and to sanction their own lively interests and enthusiasms. We will all have met someone like the boy in the remedial class who 'came to life' in his English work as soon as the teacher took an interest in the boy's accounts of the scrap-dealer's horse that he spent much of his spare time on, grooming, feeding, riding, leading through traffic, and so on. The boy had something to *give* to the teacher and to the rest of the class.

At 11+, many kids are still keenly interested in birds' nests, fishing, keeping rabbits, and similar pursuits: and the books that most frequently disappear from the school library invariably include *The Observer's Book of Birds*. In reading, both intensively and extensively, in writing, whether it be story, journal, poem or straight factual record, we must learn to capitalize on such passions — not so as to spoil them by 'officializing' them by an apparent takeover bid, but by allowing and encouraging them to permeate and inform as many aspects of 'work' as may be appropriate. The twelve year old who has just found a fledgling owl, fallen from the nest, may well be able to think of nothing else for a week or two: let him, then, find out about diet, habits, possibilities of survival, and let him keep a record of his successes and troubles in the delicate business of fostering such a creature. And let us try to ensure that the school is equipped to serve such interests and needs, rather than to ignore them or defeat them.

* Lorenz: 'It costs almost nothing and is indeed wonderful.'

If group-work or individual work is envisaged, it should be possible for pupils – *during* their English lessons – to make and record observations of animal behaviour, especially if the creatures are close at hand, in the rural-science department, in the field behind the school, or in the gutters and eaves of the school. Such work offers numerous possibilities of collaboration between English and science teachers.

Again, much observation, of the behaviour of pets especially, can take place at home: how many words, gestures, or signs does your dog understand? How many hours does he sleep during Sunday? What is the extent of his 'territory'? How does he get on with the cat next door? (Cf. the Nuffield Biology course, Book 1).

The relationship between work in English and real life should be one of a constant interplay, of reciprocal channels, so that the vivid minutiae of life as lived are fed naturally into 'English', and the stimuli and demands of 'English' intensify, extend and help to make articulate the activities and pursuits of life. Such an exchange is especially possible in work dealing with animals, since the possibility of close, attentive, controlled observation is almost always available.

Such work can of course be sustained over a period of time in the form of log-books, life-histories and so on.

### Forms

These range from casual anecdote to tightly wrought rhymes, from little jokes to sustained narrative, from accounts of amateurish excitements to careful, detailed, sustained observations by experts.

Pupils' written work done in connection with creatures can be allowed the same range of variety, both of length and form; a short 'spasm' of intensive classroom response, in the form of a short poem; and systematic recording of sustained observation of, say, flies in autumn and winter, or of the use of insecticides. Ideally, all pupils working on creatures should elect to do such work because of a prior interest which they themselves feel: their work-books should then be allowed to follow their own predilections, according to their temperaments and the rhythms of passionate preoccupation and phases of waning interest, as the weeks or months go by. In this sense, some of the best work will be 'opportunistic', as when a thirteen year old boy found an injured bird and cared for it over a period of weeks, keeping a log of its progress, diet, habits and eventual return to its natural habitat.

### A note on names

In some cases, the creature is also given its Latin name. These derive from Linnaeus's system of classification. On Linnaeus, see the *Oxford Junior Encyclopaedia*, vol 5, page 275.

### Interested parties

Pupils should be encouraged to make contact with, and invite to their lessons, local naturalists, whose names and addresses (and local publications) will be available at the local public library. Old people are also a great source of stories about childhood experiences of animals in the world of sixty years ago, before the ravages of cars and lorries and pollution.

The Royal Society for the Protection of Birds has its headquarters at The Lodge, Sandy, Beds. It is in the forefront of the battle against poisons such as D D T and other dangerous chemicals, and it needs all the support that it can get.

My warmest thanks are due to various friends, colleagues and pupils, for advice, consultation, criticism and encouragement: especially to Brian Rees-Williams; Patrick Radley and the other members of the project; Martin Lightfoot of Penguin Education; Paul Olson, Director of the Tri-University Project in Elementary Education, University of Nebraska; Alf Colley, Jack Trevena and Edwin Escritt for professional cooperation; Jackie Butler for her alert and meticulous typing; and especially to Catherine for sharing the chores and the delights.

My biggest debt as a teacher is to kids who worked with me in schools in West Bromwich, Coventry, York, Heslington, Lincoln, Nebraska and California. I hope they have enjoyed their part in the compiling of this collection. *It's to them that I'd like to dedicate it.*

# Books for the Classroom Library

Animals are a special case in many ways: there are so many books, both fiction and non-fiction, that children ought to have access to, that it is difficult to make a selection. I have compromised and made my own selection of a short list, but also included a much longer list of further reading at the end of the detailed notes.

Joan Aiken, *The Wolves of Willoughby Chase* (Puffin)

Meindert DeJong, *The Wheel on the School* (Puffin)

Philippa Pearce, *A Dog so Small* (Puffin)

E. B. White, *Charlotte's Web* (Puffin)

Henry Williamson, *Tarka the Otter* (Puffin)

Konrad K. Lorenz, *Man Meets Dog* (Penguin)

George Schaller, *The Year of the Gorilla* (Penguin)

Anthony Smith, *The Body* (Pelican)

George MacBeth (Editor), *The Penguin Book of Animal Verse* (Penguin)

Gerald Durrell, *My Family and Other Animals* (Penguin)

Rachel Carson, *The Silent Spring* (Penguin)

# Notes

### 8  Street Incident with Horse

A beautifully intriguing sequence. There's a lot to talk about here. What do the men have to do in order to get the horse and cart working again? Which of the men is taking the initiative? Are any of them aware of the photographer? Discussion may well lead into a short story or a poem.

### 9  I could have told you a lot of queer things

'. . . if I hadn't forgotten them I could have told you a lot of queer things.' How are our pupils to escape such forgetting and the losses of forgetfulness? Systematically, through work such as that in the Nuffield Biology syllabus, they can keep a record of animal and bird behaviour. Privately, for personal satisfaction, they can learn from Ted Hughes's manner of 'capturing' animals, as he explains it in 'Capturing a Fox' (see pages 18–19). Hudson's passage provides a good occasion for asking, 'What do *you* remember? And you? About tadpoles? Fishing? Flies?'

### 10  The Hedgehog

An early attempt, written before the establishment of biology or zoology as systematic sciences, to describe the distinctive characteristics of a particular species. Pupils will enjoy distinguishing between (a) genuine first-hand observation (b) hearsay (e.g. the Egyptian mice). For these two elements, see Anthony Thwaite's poem, on page 11.

### 11  Hedgehog

Cf. John Clare's poem in *Voices*, volume 1, no. 99. '. . . just where the drain pipe clogs . . .' One of the virtues of this sort of poem is that it provokes us to re-examine our familiar environment, to see it afresh, to notice creatures that we may otherwise overlook or ignore. Hedgehogs turn up even in the most apparently unpromising environments, and pupils in urban schools should be encouraged to keep an eye open. And what other surprises lurk in the backyard? Under the floorboards?

John Hewitt also has an excellent poem on finding a hedgehog (in *Collected Poems*, MacGibbon & Kee).

### 11  Hedgehogs in Heaven

Which creatures will be in *your* heaven?
On gypsies and animals, see:
John Sampson, *The Wind on the Heath* (Chatto & Windus)
Jean Paul Clébert, *Gypsies* (Penguin) and
*Gypsies and Other Travellers* (HMSO)
which will dispel all sentimental illusions about the 'glamour' of their lives.

## 12    Found Poem: The Menagerie at Versailles in 1775

A beautiful example of an acute observer in the act of 'thinking aloud':
get pupils to isolate the moments at which they are thinking, speculating,
about what they see, moments of surprise and moments of specially
intense pleasure.

## 12–13    The Menagerie

Has the artist taken liberties with his subject? Surely all these animals
could not be all together in the same enclosure? How many can your
pupils identify?

## 14    The Locust

It's interesting to compare these comparisons with those in the next
passage. The poem provides an excellent 'model' for the pupils' own
writing. What was it like? 'It was like . . . and its head was like . . .'
The more distinctive a creature is, the more we depend on comparisons
with familiar things in describing it.

## 15–17    The Soft Voice of the Serpent

It's worth exploring this closely: close observation gives rise to discovery
of the unexpected or unsuspected ('He had never realized . . .'); an
interesting play with meanings of words, with concepts: what *is* a 'body'?
When is a body not a body? When are legs not legs? The observer falls
back on comparisons to clarify in his mind what he sees, and, noticing its
likeness to a man mopping his brow, he 'began to feel enormously
interested in the creature'. Then a 'general' similarity becomes very
particular: like him, it has lost a leg. And so, surprisingly, he laughs:
a laughter of the exhilaration of recognition? The woman's reactions
are equally complicated – guilt, horror, nervousness, pity. Finally, the
man's irritation – for the fact that, unlike the locust, he cannot fly, or
for the fact that the woman has driven it away?

Interesting to contrast this man's way of observing, which involves feeling
and identification, with Topsell's or Tinbergen's.

## 18    Capturing a Fox

In my experience, 'The Thought-Fox' has never failed to intrigue pupils of
ten and over: as a result of reading it, they seem to be more interested in
thinking and talking about two things: creatures moving, on the outside;
and how thoughts come to themselves, on the inside. The interior
phenomenon they find peculiarly interesting: where do thoughts come
from? Which kinds of thoughts come quickly, unbidden? Which come
slowly and with difficulty? In talking and writing about these questions,
they also use analogies, some in the form of creatures, and others in the
form of natural phenomena, like lightning and storms; e.g.

**Thought-Storm**

Brewing up far beyond the clouds,
The thunderstorm boils,
Thundering far away from the old tree.

Getting nearer to its prey,
Hunting, haunting, hovering,
Nearer, and nearer.

Till, suddenly, with one great flash of inspiration,
The tree is struck,
The thunder drives the tree home to the ground permanently.

*Tom Morgan (age 12)*

## 20 Mass Killings

Tinbergen's *Tracks* is one of the most fascinating documents ever produced on animals in their environments. So far in this book we have had close observation and hearsay; to these is now added the act of drawing intelligent conclusions, of recreating an event – rather in the manner of a detective – on the basis of the remnants of evidence. Mud, sand and snow provide particularly good surfaces for this forensic art.

## 22 Leeuwenhoek Discovers 'Little Animals'

Here is what Anthony Smith has to say of van Leeuwenhoek:

The first man to see bacteria and protozoa, the first to see red blood corpuscles, and the first to describe the insect's compound eye was also the first man to see spermatozoa. Living a simple life as a rich merchant of Delft, Anthony van Leeuwenhoek spent much of his ninety-one years constructing his own microscopes, grinding his own lenses and then looking through them at the far more miniature world beyond them. His microscopes looked more like a draughtsman's compasses than optical instruments, but they could magnify by some 160 times. Therefore they could unlock much of the invisible world beyond the normal reach of the human eye.

It was in 1677 that he and his friend L. Hamm looked at human semen, and saw minute objects swimming in it. The Royal Society of London was then very new, having been formed the moment political stability and Charles II returned to England, but it was the leading scientific society in the world, and the Dutch microscopist sent it a letter detailing his findings. Simultaneously, bearing in mind the fact that human semen might be considered an indelicate subject for discussion, he begged the Society not to publish his findings should it consider them either obscene or immoral. The Society found them fascinating, and published without delay. The existence of human spermatozoa has therefore been known for almost 300 years (*The Body,* Penguin).

For more information of Leeuwenhoek, see Dobell, *Anthony van Leeuwenhoek and His Little Animals* (Constable). For a brief account of animalcules, see Charles Singer, *A Short History of Scientific Ideas,* page 283 (OUP).

## 24 Observing Flies

(For further information on flies, see C. N. Colyer and C. O. Hammond: *Flies of the British Isles* (Warne), and the British Museum Booklet: *The House-Fly as a Danger to Health* (British Museum).)

The style of Gilbert White's record strikes me as admirably vivid and forceful – the closeness of his observation gets into the language, and his intense interest is readily felt.

Get some pupils to observe the behaviour of flies in their living-rooms at home, their routes, their favourite places for food or rest, their persistence in the face of 'shooing'. Watch a fly in the classroom; try to predict its behaviour.

### 26    The Naming of Insects

Pupils enjoy creating their own names. Here, they can try to match names to insects, and explore the ways in which the phonological structures of words have particular characteristics suggesting lightness, weight, delicacy, fragility and so on.

### 27    At the Housefly Planet

A theme that is often explored, for horrific ends, in science-fiction films. Here it is turned to a joke. The joke in line 11 depends on knowing children's names for certain kinds of food: e.g., 'flies' cemetery' for currant loaf. English lessons are diminished by the exclusion of such inventiveness.

### 27    The Wanton Boy

This raises nice questions of emotional responses: wanton killing of flies may well be a sympton of a destructive animosity which can be fed by assumed animosity coming in the opposite direction from the creatures. Blake is careful *not* to say that the spider feels enmity toward the boy; the enmity which the boy feels to be directed toward himself is of his own making.

### 27    Haiku (We listen to insects)

Interesting to discuss how far, in what ways, this is true. At night, for example, when we can hear faint mosquito noises, and the muffled drone of human voices: one threatening, the other . . .?

### 28–9    Man and Spider

Did the spider eventually do what the man wanted him to do? Is the man satisfied at the end? If not, what does his posture suggest? Is it that he cannot now put his shoe back on?

### 30    A Chorale of Cherokee Night Music

Ask your pupils if the sequence of names, after the title, corresponds to the sequence of sounds; e.g. Does the screech-owl say 'wahuhu'? The goose say 'sasa'?

The chickadee is a titmouse which says, also, 'chickadee'; the katydid a form of locust, its name also being 'echoic'.

A beautiful poem for performance: the night sky is full of the sounds of creatures, buzzing, whirring, sawing, singing and so on. It can be performed *pianissimo* if your classroom walls are thin. When working on performances of this poem, with pupils both in England and in America, I have found them to be surprisingly inhibited, after about twelve years old, about making animal sounds. One way round this shyness is to have a small group of friends make a tape-recording independently of oneself. Technically, the challenge is to find a satisfactory half-way house between word and sound.

### 31    Orgy

The ant-eater, excited by hunger, hurtles with great speed through its meal, in a frenzy of ravenousness. An ideal poem for reading aloud at a breakneck pace. Leave pupils to read it first for themselves, and puzzle it out. You might, at some point, ask them how many letters Edwin Morgan limited himself to:

*a* b *c* d *e* f g h i j k l m *n o* p q *r s t u* v w x y z.

So, paradoxically, he has created an impression of greedy disorder by restricting himself to only eight letters of the alphabet.

## 32 Boy and a Butterfly

The notation of close observation provides one sort of pleasure, but many pupils move irresistibly toward narration so as to give 'shape' to the experience.

An excellent and inspiring adjunct to this poem is Marcel Marceau's film, *Pantomimes*, which contains a breathtaking butterfly-catcher sequence.

## 33 Talking to a Butterfly

Was Solomon, then, mad, or was he wise even in this? Pupils are always interested in communicating with their pets and are happy to explore the differences between this kind of almost one-way communication and conversation between people.

## 33 Haiku (The butterfly), Haiku (Sneezing)

Fragmentary perceptions such as these testify to the usefulness of notebooks. Yayu's haiku is particularly acute, since the eye only too easily loses the rising lark.

## 34 Feel Like a Bird

The appropriateness of 'star-toes' is appreciated if one recalls the footprints of birds on snow. In the fifth stanza, the 'quartered apple' image is useful in creating a visual clue to the way in which the two eyes of the bird look out in two directions and produce a wide stereoscopic view of 'the scene before'. In the last stanza the 'muffled shoulders' are the bird's own shoulders: it is at the wing-root that the bird's musculature is most distinctive, over-developed – by human standards – in order to provide lift. Muffled: thickly feathered; like a muffler, providing cover and warmth; also muffling sound, as in predatory birds, who depend on near-silence for surprise.

Notice the way that May Swenson has written in a kind of shorthand as if she was concentrating so hard on 'feeling like a bird' that she could only make the briefest of verbal notations, not wasting a word.

Pupils who get 'hooked' by this poem should be encouraged to look at a masterpiece of popularization: Richard Cromer: *The Miracle of Flight* (Doubleday). This book, beautifully illustrated, drew on the expert advice of Emmet Blake, Curator of Birds at the Chicago Natural History Museum, and of Alan Cromer, Associate Professor of Physics, Northeastern University. Like Anthony Smith's *The Body*, it represents the epitome of supremely intelligent and exciting popularization.

## 34–5 Cockatoo Flying

Each line of photographs should be read horizontally, so as to follow the movement of the bird. An American, Eadweard Muybridge, is the most famous of the photographers who, for the first time in history, captured the true movements of animals and birds in motion: his experiments started in 1870 with an argument about how a horse actually moved its legs, and culminated in his book *Animal Locomotion* (1887). For further information on Muybridge and on his French counterpart, Etienne Marey, see Helmut and Alison Gernsheim: *A Concise History of Photography* (Thames & Hudson).

Get pupils to find a word for each moment of movement of the wings – swoosh, flop, flap, flick, etc. and so compose a serial poem.

### 36    Heron

A poem written for this volume in response to an invitation which included the photograph on page 37.
fossicker: rummager
oystercatchers: distinctively noisy birds, especially when disturbed.

### 38    The Raven

If it is possible to provide pupils with a camera, the kind of focusing of attention that is involved in composing photographs has beneficial effects on the demands they make of themselves in their talking and writing.

### 40    Rook-Shooting, The Fire Engine and the Jackdaws

The virtue of Kilvert's writing – its unaffectedness – is due in part to the fact that he was writing for his own eyes alone. He seems never to have been bored or blasé. Is it possible for us occasionally to replicate these conditions in our pupils?

### 41    The Chaffinch Map of Scotland

This poem is based on a distribution map of Scots dialect names for the chaffinch. Younger pupils enjoy performing it aloud, and many display considerable ingenuity in composing nick-name 'maps' or plans of their classrooms and of staff-rooms.

### 42    Tadpole Time

To write as one actually talks is *extremely* difficult, but to achieve certain kinds of authenticity, it becomes necessary; certainly, the vividness of Barry Hines's story derives a lot from the 'speaking' voice. Pupils, trying this sort of thing, invariably diverge in the direction of 'correctness' and formality.

### 45    I am the Slowworm

The solitariness, independence and privacy of the creature are savoured with something like envy, by some pupils. Even more enjoy the sensuous richness of the wet autumnal landscape.

### 47    Snakes

vulgar: of the people, as opposed to scholars
furze kidders: people who collect furze as fuel for their fires
nimble: move nimbly
pilling: peeling or stripping
french prisoners: during the Napoleonic wars; the models (of ships, etc.) that they made during captivity can still be seen in Peterborough Museum.

'Tadpole Time' is a conscious effort to write talk; Clare seems to write unconsciously in a manner close to his speech-patterns. Pupils may care to comment on the degree to which his lack of punctuation makes reading difficult.

**49    Snake-Phobia**

herpetologist: a reptile-expert

Much of the fascination of this lies in its unusual degree of honesty: 'everthing I thought I knew . . . was absolutely wrong'. Our pupils may, for various reasons, find it more difficult to be so honest: they will nevertheless have their hoard of more or less nonsensical 'old wives' tales' and phobias.

**58    The Cave**

The panic in Moorehead's account derives in part from a sense of being overwhelmed by superior cunning, sheer deadliness, and overwhelming numbers. 'The Cave', like 'A Country Matter' and 'Buzzing Death', is more concerned with the last of these.

**60    A Country Matter**

The poem is like an answer to the question, breaking in on his nightmare memory, 'What's the matter?' Pupils will be interested in discussing the reactions of his fellow-pupils and teachers.

**60    The Hornet**

twud = toad = *any* unpleasant creature (West Country).

**61    Buzzing Death**

The distinctively formal, almost legal, tone of this story (e.g. 'My timely rescue was effected . . .') seems to heighten, rather than diminish, its effectiveness: a genuinely sensational event recounted in an unsensational way. Best to read this *aloud.*

**63    Bee Beard**

The queen-bee has been placed on the man's chin, and the swarm have gathered around her. The man has been stung so often that he is, by now, immune to bee stings. Not recommended for beginners.

**64    Haiku (The aged dog)    How so?**

**64    Esther's Tomcat**

Ted Hughes wrote this poem for a friend, Esther: hence the title.

**65    The Pet Shop**

The characters with the wild birds, at the end of the poem, unable to afford to buy a bird from the shop, make do with wild birds. In some areas, they are still sold 'under the counter'. Many of us find the pet-shop irresistible, even if only to indulge our fantasies or feast our eyes.

## 65 Bird Drama

How many birds can you detect? And what exactly is the 'drama'?

## 66 French Persian Cats having a Ball

A favourite poem with my pupils, both for performing aloud and for interpreting and arguing about. The sounds that the poem makes suggest both the sounds of cat's paws on polished floors and the rhythms of the dance. The patterns that the poem makes suggest both dance formations and also the patterns of a persian carpet.

I have used this poem with twenty different classes, ages ranging from eight to sixteen, and with fifteen different groups of teachers, both in England and America. No two groups have ever produced the same performance. Some are very delicate and muted, others wildly noisy and abandoned. Some sounded like humans, others like cats.

## 67 The Parson's Eye-Lid and the Black Cat's Tail, Mending the Cat

Two sides of a cat-lover: credulity and pragmatism, or superstition and cool-nerved practicality. Neither is offered as an example for imitation to one's pupils!

## 68 Horse

The poem, a series of brilliant images, belongs to the Scottish islands.

burn: stream

In its simplicity, the poem provides an ideal 'model' for students' writing about their creatures; e.g. the cat on the hearth, the cat on the roof, the cat in the backyard, the cat in the basket, the cat on the lap, the cat on the wall.

## 68 The Horse

Here is what a very bright pupil wrote after being aroused by this celebration of the horse:

### Fox

There was a rustle then a bark
In the bushes ahead of me.
It is the chicken-hunter.
His nostrils quiver and his ears prick.
He smells the hen-house afar off.
Who has provided him with his lissom movements?
Can you make him as timid as a young deer?
Who has given him his Machiavellian thoughts?
He jeers at fear.
Slyly he jeopardizes the safety of his prey.
The hunt does not affright him.
He is an invulnerable creature,
Can he not challenge the fastest hare in the country?

*Heather Doloughan (age 12)*

## 69 Study of a Horse

Leonardo's drawing captures, through its multiple images, the movement of the horse's head. Cf. the note on pages 34—5, and, for similar effects, see the work of Marinetti and other Italian 'Futurist' painters. See Aaron Scharf: *Art and Photography* (Allen Lane The Penguin Press).

### 71 The Uses of Animals

Pupils will be able to offer other examples of the way in which animals serve to vivify idioms and folk-lore, in simile, metaphor, and proverb.

### 72 Song of the Battery Hen, Is it cruel? Or isn't it?

Three contributions to the continuing debate about intensive breeding and farming, in which creatures are removed from anything remotely like their natural habitat and are placed in a totally artificial, mechanically controlled environment in the interests of larger profit-margins. Criticisms tend to be almost exclusively anthropomorphic, assuming that animals 'suffer' in the same way as human beings.

### 74 Hanno and Ping

Here Ping, the displaced Chinese boy, meets Hanno, the displaced gorilla, 'degraded, as in a slum'. Subsequently, they enjoy a remarkable friendship. On the whole question of animals in cages, see Lorenz: *King Solomon's Ring.*

### 78 Finding the Gorilla

For over a century, the gorilla has been the subject of a great deal of myth-making: George Schaller was provoked to find out the truth. His findings contain many surprises; one of the distinctive virtues of his account is that he observed the gorillas at close quarters in their own natural environment, without interfering with them or capturing them.

### 80 Wolves Fighting

Pupils will be able to apply this to their own observation of dogs fighting in the street.

### 82 How to Talk to Elephants

Doubtless, nothing more than a pleasant coincidence, but well deserved, nevertheless. How do people talk to dogs, cats, canaries?

### 83 Elephants are Different to Different People

Pupils will enjoy trying to decide whom they most resemble of these three. They can also add more voices to the conversation.

### 83, 84–5 Elephant, A Mammoth Woodcut

These drawings exemplify Sandburg's point that elephants are different to different people. One is sinuous, smooth, delicate, all fine lines and movement, while the other is richly featured.

### 86 Pygmies' Elephant Song

Pupils can usefully speculate on the *purposes* of this song in the context of the hunt, and compare it with occasions, in our culture, when people feel it needful or appropriate to sing.

### 87  Orpingalik's Song: My Breath

C. M. Bowra's note on this song is:

The main text is sung by the leader, and the refrain by his companions in the chase. . . . Songs with refrains arise from the desire to combine individual performance with communal interest. . . . They allow full play to the creative song-maker and to the company whose feelings he shares and expresses.

There are two very fine records of Eskimo songs and dances:
The Eskimos of Hudson Bay and Alaska (Ethnic Folkways Library, FE 4444).
Eskimo Songs from Alaska (Ethnic Folkways Library, FE 4069).
In the notes to FE 4444, Laura Bolton writes:

One man, when asked how many songs he had, answered: 'I have many. Everything in me is song. I sing as I breathe.'
Another singer said: 'Music makes the old young, and the drum is the beating heart.'

FE 4069 includes Helicopter Song; Rise Up, Helicopter, Like a Bird; and Eskimo Rock'n'Roll.

### 95  Hyena

Like *Heron,* this poem was written for this volume in response to an invitation. The suspense and tension of the poem, its threatening quality, begins in the first line and is sustained right through to the end, even within the hyena's state of relaxation.

### 97  The Third Day of the Wolf

Much of the best animal-literature of the recent past has been, in effect, 'a wreath for wildness'. Many species have become extinct or almost so, during the past hundred years, as a result of the activities of 'civilized man', the bison and the carrier pigeon to name but two. Even now, the caribou of the far North of America are threatened by the opening up of the Alaskan oil-fields. If the caribou are destroyed, the Eskimos also will be destroyed. This poem is based on an actual incident, when a wolf escaped from a zoo; he appears in the photograph on page 99.

### 100  The Ghost of the Buffaloes

Vachel Lindsay's romantic regret for the disappearance of magnificent wild life is mixed with an almost inescapable failure to appreciate, to understand, the culture of the North American Indian: their 'gibbering' is simply how *he* hears them: to them, *his* talk would be mere gibbering.

### 104  Men have been in our woods and have killed our badgers

The sequel to Judith Cook's article and the publicity that this gave to the children's campaign was described in a further article by Miss Cook, in the *Guardian,* 29 March 1968, entitled 'Saving the badgers'. It read:

When I last went to St Gorran School on the Helford River, in Cornwall, to write about the children and the death by baiting of their badgers it was high summer. This time the weather was again warm, a golden day common to the early Cornish spring, and although the trees were bare the daffodils were out and the water in the river was bright blue, an effect of the clarity of the light peculiar to this time of year.

I went to see how the children were getting on, whether they had discovered who killed their badgers, and what precautions they were taking to see it did not happen again. 'Oh, we know who did it now', said one of the mistresses, 'but we just can't prove it. Anyway, the children are now fencing off the whole creek; it seems a pity, but it's the only way.' Fencing off the creek has proved expensive, but the work is coming on well.

Following my article, the children received some £25 from *Guardian* readers ('It took us a week to answer them all, we sort of shared the work out. . . .'). A cheque for £50 came from another, Spike Milligan, and there were more amounts from readers of the local press. The children raised £36 10s. themselves doing jobs. After they had put up the first length of fence they realized it would not be sufficient and so got to work again.

### Earning the money
This time they needed £12. So far they have had money from B B C television viewers who watched a programme on badgers, an anonymous donation from an old lady who said she would double what the children had already earned, and to date the children have earned another £27 themselves. 'We need £40 to finish it, but we'll do it', said one small girl. 'Children don't get paid much, though, it takes *ages*.' To earn the money the children have hired themselves out to local villages as gardeners, log cutters, wood sellers and cleaners. They have made seed compost from their woodland leaf mould, baskets out of willow and have recaned stools and chairs.

But the children are still worried. A letter appeared in the local paper from a man signing himself 'Gamekeeper' ('He's not,' said one of the children, 'we know who he is and he's a rabbit snarer'), couched in dramatic terms, telling of the dangers of badgers; of innocent cyclists attacked on their way home from work by savage badgers; and the irresponsibility of children who run across the setts and cause the badgers to turn wild, kill their young and destroy their homes. He speaks of the feeling of work well done as he and his friends settle down for a few pints after a badger dig. It is not by chance that this letter appeared now, for Good Friday marks the start of the badger-baiting season (as I said last time, there are strange practices connected with badgers and Easter Sunday).

The children answered the letter refuting all the points made and saying that they feel a few pints of beer must indeed have been drunk by those innocent villagers attacked by badgers. All wild animals are savage, if attacked, they say, especially in the mating season. So far from children causing badgers to destroy their young, the St Gorran badgers accepted the children, who watched quietly while the cubs played.

'We children did not make the badger dig itself out of its sett with a steel spade and tear its mate to death. This was done by men.'

### Lord Stonham's advice
They do not feel that their campaign to make the badger a protected species has gone well so far. Lord Stonham, at the Home Office, referred them to a book, 'Predatory Mammals', and on his advice they showed it to the local badger hunters, but 'they just laughed a lot, used bad language, and refused to read it.'

The children say they cannot understand why 'the Government won't do what you ask them'! They are continuing with their efforts through work and the press ('Who writes to the *Guardian* editor?' 'I do,' says Morris, aged eleven). 'Please tell the readers we're very grateful,' says the twelve-year-old girl who organized it all. 'I expect some of us will take it when we're older.'

A procession of children led us down to the sett and the creek discussing how they had worked on the fencing. I have come across few children so articulate and so concerned. 'We had difficulty with him,' the headmistress had said to me earlier, pointing out one of the party. 'He came to us after committing a serious offence; no one wanted him. Do you know, we had to teach him how to be affectionate, how to love.' These children certainly have a real and abiding love for wild life, but they are not very happy about human beings. This spring badger-baiting dogs are being imported from Ireland.

As they say in their latest letter to Lord Stonham, 'The book isn't working, is it, sir?'

**106  Anonymous: 'It's a marvellous sport and not at all cruel'**

Part of a continuing debate that can usefully enter the classroom.

**111  Creepers and Crawlers**

The Insect Play offers many opportunities for improvisation and for spirited performance. The whole play is available in an OUP paperback edition.

**116  Boasting**

Just two examples of the great wealth of boasts to be found in the American tall-tale, or tall-story, oral tradition.

**117  Wilderness**

What do our pupils think is inside *them*? This is an ideal way of describing one's own various facets without depending on an abstract or over-simple psychological vocabulary.

Carl Sandburg may conceivably have been drawing on the folk-tradition seen in Colonel Davy Crockett's boasting.

**118  To a Fish**

This serves as an amusing and thought-provoking 'model' for the pupil's own dialogues, with canaries, budgerigars, cats, dogs, maggots, etc.

**120  Dunce Song**

Van Doren's use of the word 'intelligent' is, of course, ironic. If our pupils also wish sometimes that they were animals, what are *their* reasons? Freedom? Indolence? Irresponsibility? Glamour?

Mark Van Doren provided his own explanation when he read the poem at a conference held in the Library of Congress, Washington, DC.

**121  Palmstroem in Animal Costume**

A good opportunity for exploring the common animal metaphors in current uses: 'You cheeky monkey, you!', 'Greedy pig!', etc.

Palmstroem is a character who appears in many of Morgenstern's poems.

**122  The End**

Pupils may well have attempted similar crazy experiments, on however modest a scale; this is a rich field for fantasy, day-dreams and dreams.

**Classification of extracts by subject**
(numbers refer to pages)

| Observing | Hunting and Exploiting | Protecting |
|---|---|---|
| 8 | 18–19 | 11 |
| 9 | 27 | 67 |
| 10 | 40 | 104–9 |
| 12–13 | 42–3 | |
| 15–17 | 72–3 | |
| 20–21 | 74–6 | |
| 22–3 | 86 | |
| 24 | 87–9 | |
| 33 | 97–9 | |
| 34–5 | | |
| 38–9 | | |
| 78–82 | | |
| 118–19 | | |

| Tall Stories and Fantasy | Revulsions and Fears | For Performance |
|---|---|---|
| 9 | 14 | 30 |
| 11 | 15–17 | 31 |
| 26 | 42–3 | 36–7 |
| 27 | 49–57 | 41 |
| 47–8 | 58–9 | 66 |
| 111–15 | 60 | 100–103 |
| 116 | 61–2 | |
| 120–22 | 95–6 | |

# Further Reading

## Fiction for the pupil

Joan Aiken, *Night Birds on Nantucket* (Cape), *The Wolves of Willoughby Chase* (Cape).
May d'Alencon, *Red Renard* (ULP).
Katherine Allfrey, *On a Dolphin's Back* (Methuen).
Richard and Florence Attwater, *Mr Popper's Penguins* (Bodley Head).
Gillian Avery, *The Elephant War* (Collins).

H. Mortimer Batten, *The Singing Forest* (Blackwood).
Michel-Aime Baudouy, *Bruno, King of the Wild* (Bodley Head).
Hans Baumann, *I Marched with Hannibal* (OUP).
Paul Berna, *The Mule on the Motorway* (Bodley Head).
Lucy M. Boston, *A Stranger at Green Knowe* (Faber).
Reidar Brodtkorb, *Flying Free* (Methuen).

W. H. Canaway, *Sammy Going South* (Penguin).
Richard Coe, *Doctor Concocter* (OUP).
D. A. Cramer-Schaap, *Uncle Boom-la-la* (Methuen).
F. D. Davison, *Man-Shy* (Puffin).
Meindert DeJong, *The Little Cow and the Turtle* (Lutterworth), *Shadrach* (Lutterworth), *Along Came a Dog* (Lutterworth), *Hurry Home, Candy* (Lutterworth), *The Wheel on the School* (Puffin).

Phyllis R. Fenner (Editor), *Elephants, Elephants, Elephants* (Chatto & Windus), *Horses, Horses, Horses* (Chatto & Windus).

Helen Griffiths, *The Wild Horse of Santander* (Hutchinson), *Leon* (Hutchinson).
René Guillot, *Fonabis and the Lion* (Harrap), *The Wild White Stallion* (Harrap), *Grichka and Brother Bear* (ULP), *The Animal Kingdom* (OUP).

Richard Hughes, *The Spider's Palace and other Stories* (Chatto & Windus).

Will James, *Smoky* (Puffin).
Alan C. Jenkins (Editor), *Animal Stories* (Blackie).
Nicholas Kalashnikoff, *The Defender* (OUP).
N. Karazin, *Cranes Flying South* (Longman).
Rudyard Kipling, *The Two Jungle Books* (Macmillan), *Collected Dog Stories* (Macmillan), *All the Mowgli Stories* (Macmillan).

Evelyn Sibley Lampman, *The City under the Back Steps* (Faber).
Andrew Lang, *The Animal Story Book* (Longman).

Rutherford Montgomery, *Carcajou* (Longman), *Kildee House* (Faber), *Mister Jim* (Faber), *Flossie and Bossie* (Faber).

Robin Palmer, *Dragons, Unicorns and other Magical Beasts* (Hamish Hamilton).
M. E. Patchett, *Tiger in the Dark* (Brockhampton).

Philippa Pearce, *A Dog So Small* (Puffin).
Sheena Porter, *Deerfold* (OUP).
John B. Prescott, *Mountain-Lion* (Deutsch).
Marie Sandoz, *The Horsecatcher* (Brockhampton).
David Severn, *Foxy-Boy* (Bodley Head).
David Stephen, *Rory the Roebuck* (Bodley Head), *String Lug the Fox* (Lutterworth).
Ingvald Svinsaas, *Tom in the Mountains* (OUP).

James Thurber, *Thurber's Dogs* (Penguin).
Mary Treadgold, *We Couldn't Leave Dinah* (Puffin).
Henry Treece, *War Dog* (Brockhampton).

Christopher Webb, *Quest of the Otter* (Macdonald).
E. B. White, *Charlotte's Web* (Puffin).
Leon Whitney, *Pigeon City* (Ward).
Laura Ingalls Wilder, *Little House in the Big Woods* (Puffin), *Little House on the Prairie* (Puffin), *On the Banks of Plum Creek* (Puffin).
Henry Williamson, *Tarka the Otter* (Puffin), *Salar the Salmon* (Faber), *The Henry Williamson Animal Saga* (Macdonald) (includes 'The Epic of Brock the Badger').

## Fiction for the teacher to read aloud

Ray Bradbury, *The Golden Apples of the Sun* (Corgi), *Dandelion Wine* (Corgi).
William Faulkner, *The Bear* (Penguin).
Nadine Gordimer, *The Soft Voice of the Serpent and Other Stories* (Penguin).
Ernest Hemingway, *The Old Man and the Sea* (Penguin), *The Essential Hemingway* (Penguin).
Ted Hughes, *The Rain Horse* (in *Wodwo*) (Faber).
Doris Lessing, *A Sunrise on the Veld* (Panther), *Locusts* (Panther).
Patrick O'Brian, *The Last Pool and Other Stories* (Secker & Warburg).
William Saroyan, *Best Stories of William Saroyan* (Faber).
John Steinbeck, *Tortilla Flat* (Penguin).
Mark Twain, *The Celebrated Jumping Frog of Calaveras County* (Filter).
John Wain, *The Pig Man* (in *Nuncle and Other Stories*) (Penguin).

## Non-fiction
((a) more suitable for reference; (b) more suitable for extensive reading)

(a) Millais, *The Mammals of Great Britain* (Longman).
(b) Konrad Z. Lorenz, *King Solomon's Ring* (Methuen), *On Aggression* (Cape).
(a) T. H. White, *The Book of Beasts* (Cape).
(b) Rachel Carson, *The Silent Spring* (Penguin).
(b) George Ewart Evans, *The Horse in the Furrow* (Faber).
(b) David Lack, *The Robin* (Witherby).
(a) E. Sandars, *A Beast Book for the Pocket* (OUP).
(a) Ernest Neal, *Badgers in Woodlands* (HMSO), *The Badger* (Collins).
(a) A. Ross, *Insects in Britain* (Blackwell).
(a) R. Taylor, *Hedgehogs, Squirrels and Dormice* (Methuen).
(b) E. D. H. Johnson, *The Poetry of Earth* (Gollancz).
(a) R. S. R. Fitter, *Birds of Town and Village* (Collins).
(a) Gilbert White, *The Natural History of Selborne* (OUP).

(b) Gerald Durrell, *My Family and Other Animals* (Penguin).
(b) Maurice Sendak, *Where the Wild Things Are* (Bodley Head).
(b) Gavin Maxwell, *The Ring of Bright Water* (Methuen).
(b) Alan Wykes, *Snake Man, The Story of C. J. P. Ionides* (Hamish Hamilton).
(b) Arthur Grimble, *A Pattern of Islands* (Murray).
(b) Hans Hass, *Diving to Adventure* (Arrow Books).
(b) George Orwell, *Shooting an Elephant* (Penguin).
(b) Thor Heyerdahl, *Kon-Tiki* (Allen & Unwin).
(b) T. H. White, *The Goshawk* (Penguin).
(a) Monica Shorten, *Squirrels* (Collins).
(a) V. J. Stanek, *The Pictorial Encyclopedia of the Animal Kingdom* (Hamlyn).
(a) Colin Clair, *Unnatural History* (Abelard-Schuman).
(b) Frantisek Vopat and Julius Komarek, *Introducing Animals* (Spring Books).
(a) E. M. Nicholson, *Birds and Men* (Collins).
(a) Bruce Campbell, *Finding Nests* (Collins).
(a) *The Oxford Junior Encyclopaedia, volume 2: Natural History* (OUP).
(a) & (b) Anthony Smith, *The Body* (Penguin). This is the best popular work on the human body; it is a brilliant piece of work, beautifully and often wittily written, and an inexhaustible treasury of extraordinary facts about that part of ourselves which we most obviously share with the lower animals.
(b) George Schaller, *The Year of the Gorilla* (Penguin).

### Poetry

John Clare, *Selected Poetry and Prose,* edited by Eric Robinson and Geoffrey Summerfield (OUP).
Geoffrey Summerfield (Editor), *Voices* (Penguin). The First Book, Nos. 65–100.
Leila Berg (Editor), *Four Feet and Two* (Puffin).
James Reeves, *Prefabulous Animiles* (Heinemann).
George MacBeth (Editor), *Penguin Book of Animal Verse* (Penguin).
John Clare, *The Shepherds Calendar*, edited by Eric Robinson and Geoffrey Summerfield (OUP).
John Hewitt, *Collected Poems* (MacGibbon & Kee).

# Family and School
## David Jackson

After several years of being processed and polythened, having learnt to mimic an academic jargon and to look upon himself as a failure because he hasn't gone on to do research, a B.Ed. or become a creative artist, the new teacher arrives at his first job. He has forgotten what he was like as a twelve year old with spitting contests, collections of bubble-gum cards, conkers, dens and dares. Very often his training has ingrained habits of language, tone and feeling which separate him from the children he is trying to teach. Defensive authoritarian attitudes frequently arise at this stage from a refusal to dredge up from within the common ground upon which he can connect to the children. An honest act of imaginative sympathy with the children is demanded, without ever patronizing them. As English teachers we must look out for the memory, joke, picture, shared story that suddenly makes the group one. And as family and school experiences form the greater part of an eleven to thirteen year old's life and memory this theme is offered as a help to bridging the teacher's and the pupils' worlds.

Keep sending them home – to Mum, to Dad, to the family, at meals quarrelling, having a laugh, going out, buying something. Then what happens? They are dealing with a situation rich in first-hand feeling, charged associations and personal relationships, alive with people they know extraordinarily well, down to the last foible. Because they know and *feel* about these things they have the language to write about them.*

Harold Rosen is right; truly involved writing, talking, acting from the children usually comes from a concern with their immediate surroundings. This is what this book is trying to do – to be on the children's side, working-class as well as middle-class children, in their play, work, relationships and humour, within their family and at school, so that any child opening the book for the first time should feel, when he sees the photograph on page 97 of the boy sulking outside the classroom door after having been sent out of a lesson, or recognizes instantly the feeling of sinking humiliation in the extract 'First day at school' by Richard Wright, 'That could be me!' The ten pieces of children's writing are meant to reinforce this impression; that the book is about responding directly and honestly to the confusion and evasions practised on them by the adult world, as in 'Seeing a parent cry for the first time'. (Children's own lore and language from the Opies' books also help the child to relate his own experience to the book through the riddles, the sayings, the trick problems and their special language for things, like school dinners.)

However there are many dangers inherent in this approach. Relevance can encourage, if taken too far and without variation, a limited vision of the world, both in language and thought. Some children can churn out, to

* Harold Rosen in *English versus Examinations*, edited by Brian Jackson, Chatto & Windus.

order, portraits of their wrinkled grandparents without being engaged at any level of themselves. This is why the imaginative extension of each part of the book by teacher and pupil is so important. I have tried to indicate in the Notes below how one might stimulate the inventiveness and fantasy of the child in such ideas as designing a model home (pages 34–5), or a school of the future (page 38), personifying household objects (page 35), experimenting with concrete poems (page 48), or extending the idea of 'Taking the register' (page 62), to include 'registering' a whole class group in words and pictures/cartoons.

Another important way of widening out the theme is to be found in the stress I have made in the Notes on inter-disciplinary thinking. The photographs of international families (pages 26–7) cry out for the help of a geography or social-studies department, and the history department would valuably support a close look at the Edwardian and Victorian family groups (pages 32–3). Further scope for other link-ups can be found in much of the other material, such as discoveries from science from page 79; and many art connections suggest themselves, varying from cartoons, the children's own photography, to modelling family groups. Some passages in the book seem, at first glance, to deal with subjects which are too emotionally loaded for children of this age to control and accept, especially the 'Where do babies come from?' extract. However, on a closer inspection it will be found that a full, emotional involvement with the subject, more suited for a fourteen to sixteen year old, has been generally avoided. Even the boy—girl encounters are written as though they are being seen from the outside. There are no adolescent soul-searchings, but only the preliminary teasings and wary skirmishings characteristic of this age range, only the sly defensive retaliation of the boy in the 'Fanta' passage (page 5), saying: 'Girls were crazy; all girls were'.

One main emphasis of the book has been the attempt to catch the different inflections of children's voices, being witty, revelling in repartee, such as this from 'Bickering' (page 52):

'Say you're sorry', the girl demanded.
'You're sorry', Sid said.
*'Say you're sorry.'*
'You're sorry.'
The girl stamped her foot.

Also, being aggressive ('You and whose army?'), and above all just being a spontaneous story-teller. Given a relaxed classroom, most children will come up with some personal anecdote connected to one of the photographs or one of the extracts, and I believe the English teacher's job is to see these contributions not as diverting red-herrings, but as of essential value. As Douglas Barnes says,

those children who come up from primary school ready to explore personal experience aloud and to offer anecdotal contribution to discussion cease to do so within a few weeks of arrival. Clearly they learn in certain lessons that anecdotes are held by the teacher to be irrelevant (*Language, the Learner and the School,* Penguin).

Rather than impose that public, official voice, that is often required of children in writing up science experiments, we must help each child to find his own voice in his own time, as in Jacqueline Thistlethwaite's 'Serious Games' (page 47), where by telling a simple memory of playing out she shows how she explored the idea of death and loss. (Notice how the ironic reference to death at the end slips out while she's not looking '. . . and every time I went out I was teased to death by them'.) I hope this book will play some small part in helping your children to recognize their true voices.

I would very much like to hear from any teacher or child who has time to write how they are using the book, or any other impressions, comments, criticisms of the book.

I am indebted to those friends, colleagues and pupils who have taught me so much: Graham White, Michael Tucker, Myles Macdowell, John Iddon, Pat Radley, Penny Blackie, Donald Ball, Geoffrey Summerfield, Elwyn Rowlands, George Sanders, Tony and Judith Crowe, John Lindsay and Todmorden Public Library, the staff and pupils of Whitworth Comprehensive, the pupils of Settle High School, particularly the members of 2 West and 1 South (1966–7) and the pupils of Kettering Grammar School, particularly 2S and 2Q (1967–8).

# Books for the Classroom Library

Elizabeth Enright, *Saturdays* (Puffin) (and the other Melendy Family books by Elizabeth Enright available in Puffin)

Frederick Grice, *Bonnie Pit Laddie* (OUP)

John Rowe Townsend, *Gumble's Yard* (Puffin)

Laura Ingalls Wilder, *Little House in the Big Woods* (Puffin).
(In all of the seven Laura Ingalls Wilder books in Puffin there are many beautifully simple yet observant family and school scenes that get through directly to children.)

Keith Waterhouse, *There is a Happy Land* (Longman)

James Kirkup, *The Only Child* (Pergamon, Athena books)

Stan Barstow, *Joby* (Penguin)

William Mayne, *No More School* (Puffin)

Edward Blishen (Editor), *The School that I'd Like* (Penguin)

John Walmsley, *Neill and Summerhill: A Pictorial Record* (Penguin)

Reginald Maddock, *The Pit* (Collins)

Ted Hughes, *Meet my Folks* (Faber)

# Notes

Section One: Birth (pages 1–3)

8 **Slippery**

The accompanying photograph is from *Positives* by Ander and Thom Gunn (Faber). Other very useful collections of photographs for the whole theme, 'Family and School' are:
*Picture Post 1938–1950*, edited by Tom Hopkinson (Penguin).
*The Family of Man*, edited by L. Steichen (Thorpe & Porter).
*Let Us Now Praise Famous Men*, J. Agee and W. Evans (Pan).
*Shadow of Light* by Bill Brandt (Bodley Head).
*The Life and Death of St Kilda* by Tom Steel (Scottish Naturalists).
Many of Roger Mayne's photographs in *Things being Various*, edited by S. Clements, J. Dixon, L. Stratta (OUP), e.g. pages 35, 42, 44, 121, 125.
*Neill and Summerhill* by John Walmsley (Penguin).

This particular photograph and poem often stimulate detailed memories of trying to bath a soapy baby brother or sister, of family bath nights, and of general attitudes and feelings to a new arrival in the family. See the bath night photograph in *Reflections,* edited by S. Clements, J. Dixon, L. Stratta (OUP) page 15, and baby asleep photograph in *Things being Various* page 48, and photographs of a baby from birth to eighteen months from *Picture Post 1938–1950*, pages 146–51.

9 **Birth**

Birth isn't just exhilarating and traumatic for Mum; it disturbs the whole routine running of the family. New relationships, new positions within the family spring from that first cry. Children talk and write in a very involved way about being displaced (or so they see it) as the youngest and the favourite in the family, about especially wanting a brother/sister – 'I really wanted a girl, Dad . . .', about having to look after the house – 'I'd like you to make the tea for Mum if she wants it.' See *Cider with Rosie* by Laurie Lee (Penguin), pages 20–21.
An interesting African contrast on the subject of sibling jealousy is in Francis Selormey's *The Narrow Path* (Heinemann African Writers series), pages 36–8, where the jealous boy's grandmother believes that for him to bath in the new baby's left over water will take away all his bitterness.

*Other Sources*
Poems
'Baby Running Barefoot' by D. H. Lawrence (*Complete Poems*, Heinemann).
'A Baby Asleep after Pain' by D. H. Lawrence (*Complete Poems*, Heinemann).
'Mary Bly' by James Wright (*The Branch will not Break*, Longman).
'Some Sort of Nursery Song' by Peter Dale (*The Storms,* Macmillan).
'Morning Song' by Sylvia Plath (*Ariel,* Faber). Parts may be useful, although the whole poem is much too difficult.

Prose
Waiting for birth — *The Rainbow* by D. H. Lawrence, pages 75—80 (Penguin).

**10  Riddle**

The Opies' books are mines of rich things for this theme, not only *Lore and Language of School Children*, where this riddle comes from, but also *Children's Games in Street and Playground* and *The Oxford Book of Nursery Rhymes* (OUP).

**Section Two: Parents and Children (pages 10—30)**

Perhaps this section can be best introduced if we hear the parents' side first; invite sympathetic parents into our classrooms and let the children ask them what family life was like when they were eleven to thirteen year olds and how it has changed since then — how were they punished, if at all? What time did they have to be in bed by? How much help around the house did they give? How much pocket money did they have? etc. Perhaps the pupils could adapt the Home and School questionnaire on pages 108—9 to use with their parents.

If parents can't be persuaded to come in then portable tape recorders can be used. A *carefully* prepared set of questions can trigger off some valuable responses which a whole class can share and discuss afterwards.

There is another possibility (only if the school is relaxed enough) of letting the children, in pairs, use the tape recorder around the school (yes, teachers are often parents as well!). I've found willing helpers in caretakers, staff, the canteen staff, nurses, even headmasters. However it should be stressed to the children that the best tapes only come from polite, sympathetic tact and willingness to join in a really active conversation and not merely to read out prepared questions.

**10  Seeing a Parent Cry for the First Time**

The honesty of the observation in this piece — 'and talked to her in a voice that she always talked to me in when I was hurt' — serves as a model for this theme. This is what I think we should be after from the children, whether it be in writing, oral work, drama or poster work.

The sudden recognition of adult fallibility (teachers as well as parents) is often the start of independent growth in the child and pupils usually write absorbedly about the moment when they realized, for the first time, that their parents weren't gods but human beings, like themselves. See also 'Out of Hand' by Joyce Cary (*Spring Song and Other Stories*, Penguin); the first chapter of *Joby* by Stan Barstow (Penguin) (keeping the real seriousness of the reason for his mother entering hospital from Joby); 'The Schoolmaster' by Yevgeny Yevtushenko (*Every Man will Shout* edited by R. Mansfield and I. Armstrong, OUP).

*Other Sources*

Poems
'Our Father' by Ray Mathew (*Voices*, volume 2, Penguin).
'My Papa's Waltz' by Theodore Roethke (*Collected Poems*, Faber).
'Father's Gloves' by Ted Walker (*Junior Voices*, volume 4, Penguin).

'The Hob-Nailed Boots what Farver Wore', traditional (*Junior Voices*, 4, Penguin).
'Discord in Childhood' by D. H. Lawrence (*Complete Poems*, Heinemann).
'Family Group' by Ken Smith (*The Pity*, Cape).
'It's Sure to End in Tears' by Vernon Scannell (*Walking Wounded*, Eyre & Spottiswoode).
'In that Year, 1914, We Lived on the Farm' by Gary Snyder (*A Range of Poems*, Fulcrum Press).
'The Follower' by Seamus Heaney (*Voices*, volume 3, Penguin).
'My Parents Kept Me from Children who were Rough' by Stephen Spender (*Things being Various*, OUP).

Photograph
'Bedroom in West Ham' by Bill Brandt (*Shadow of Light*, Bodley Head).

Prose
Dad makes a rocking chair — *Little House in the Prairie* by Laura Ingalls Wilder, pages 131–2 (Puffin).
Father as handyman — *An Only Child* by Frank O'Connor, pages 28–31 (Macmillan).
Opening three pages of *Charlotte's Web* by E. B. White (Puffin).
The Judas Touch (collected as *The Jug* in a BBC *Listening and Writing* pamphlet, Autumn 1965) by Sean O'Faolain, from *Finest Stories of Sean O'Faolain* (Bantam Classic).
Family quarrel — *Far Out the Long Canal* by Meindert de Jong, pages 122–6 (Lutterworth).
Family quarrel — *Hell's Edge* by John Rowe Townsend (Puffin) (opening).
*Henry Moore* by Herbert Read (Thames & Hudson) (Family groups and situations, especially pages 147–8, 157–63, 174–5. Can the Art department help here on modelling, painting, drawing family groups?)

13   **Five Green Bottles**

Ray Jenkins's play first appeared in a B B C *Listening and Writing* pamphlet, Spring 1966 (and repeated Spring 1969), where he gave some background to writing this play and some very useful advice on how to go about writing your own play in *Why a Play?*

**Why a Play?**

One very hot day, ages ago, my young brother suddenly asked my mother for a button-collar shirt. Point-blank — while she was doing the washing. He was a quiet boy and for him to ask for something out of the blue like that was unusual to say the least. But he did, and, unfortunately, at that time, my mother couldn't afford it. So she wiped her hands carefully, put her wedding ring back on, and said no . . . thinking no doubt that that was the end of that. But my brother was deeply upset; this must have meant a lot to him or he wouldn't have asked; and we could all see the anger biting inside him. He asked again, and again my mother said no. The incident should have stopped there, but strangely, one by one, we all, the whole family, found ourselves taking sides — for or against the shirt. The incident grew and grew. When my father came in he flatly refused to buy the shirt because he was on my mother's side and anyway he was tired. Naturally we boys lined up against the common enemy — our parents — and later on we were stopped from going out because we'd all been too insolent. My mother repented and wanted to buy the shirt but my father said no . . . and *they* began to argue. . . . And so the whole thing spread — a simple, ordinary request flowered out until it affected our lives day by day and meal by meal for a fortnight. In the end everybody's dignity was saved by my aunt who bought the shirt herself.

This little incident stuck in my mind. I knew it was the seed for a possible play sometime in the future. But why? Why was it usable? Why was the shirt so important to my brother? Why had I retained the incident and rejected,many others? It was an ordinary enough event – so why was I sure it might make the basis for a play?

The first answer is – because it was ordinary; we know about it, it was real; we can imagine such a thing happening to us even if we haven't experienced exactly *that* situation. It involves people we can easily recognize and we also know what happens sometimes to people in such a situation. You ask for something, it's important to you, and it's refused.

But, from the point of view of making a play of it, the second reason is more important. This little 'seed' of a situation is capable of being extended in lots of directions; in other words, like a good seed, it was capable of growth. You can probably think of twenty ways in which it could grow – from your own experience.

Now, what do I mean by 'growth'? Say, for example my mother had said – 'All right, course you can have a shirt' – there'd be no play. But, because she'd said 'no' – then tensions, difficulties, oppositions started building up – and *that* is the meat of any play – how people react, how we see them reacting to a situation – how they change, or don't change, how they gradually get angry or how they mellow – why they take one point of view rather than another. Right at the root of drama is argument, dispute or tension. All this doesn't mean that plays have to be about arguments or fights – what it does mean is that it has to be about differences; and because people are different they try to convince and change each other – no matter what the story: and the fireworks begin (copyright © Ray Jenkins, 1966).

The play is energetic enough to come across even in a seated reading around the class, but if approached through improvised group drama on other family crisis-points throughout the day or the year (such as other meal times, or 'The Christmas dinner when Grandma lost her glasses', other special occasions in the family – wedding celebrations, birthday parties, a funeral, a christening). Or possibly concentrating on some of the lines in the play ('There's many a starving Chinese who'd be only too glad to finish what you leave.' 'There's a lot you youngsters today have to be thankful for. . . .' 'Mum, Mum, Mum . . . am I supposed to know everything?' 'Don't say ta, say thank you.' 'Kids. You have them, you raise them and then, one day, before you can turn around, you don't know them.') There are several ways in which the play can be fully shared and enjoyed.

The really demanding thing about this play for the teacher and eleven to thirteen year olds is to avoid the temptation of merely sending up Gramp's character for laughs and to bring out the poignancy of the bowling invitation. Here is a lonely man made to feel important and wanted again. When Gramp goes out, saying, 'I'm very happy, my dear', we should *all* feel sorry for him.

*Other Source Material on Grandparents*

'One of the virtues' by Stan Barstow (*Springboard,* edited by D. Jackson, Harrap). (Longman have recorded Barstow reading this story on *Stories on Record,* along with 'The Human Element'.)
Granny Fitch description – *A Dog so Small* by Philippa Pearce, pages 32–4 (Puffin).
Grandmother – *An Only Child* by Frank O'Connor, pages 19–20 (Macmillan).
A visit to Grandpa's – *Portrait of the Artist as a Young Dog* by Dylan Thomas (Dent) (recorded on Caedmon TC 1132).
'Still Jim and Silent Jim' by Philippa Pearce (*Another Six,* Blackwell).
Granny's sick – *Black Boy* by Richard Wright, opening pages (Longman).

Being influenced by a Grandmother – *Bonnie Pit Laddie* by Frederick Grice, page 66 (OUP).
Fighting with Grandad – *For Want of a Nail* by Melvyn Bragg, pages 60–61 (Penguin).

Poems
'My Grandmother' by Elizabeth Jennings (*Impact One*, Heinemann).

## 25, 26   Miner at his Evening Meal, Miner's Child

From *Shadow of Light* by Bill Brandt; their starkly authentic observation sensitively records a family atmosphere. Can children do the same for their own family atmosphere in photographs, paintings, words?

Photographs on international families: pages 26–7.

There's great scope here for linking up with the geography department on the contrasts in family life in different parts of the world. (If any of the BBC2 TV series on *The Family of Man* can be seen these contrasts are clearly brought out there. The 'Four Families' – Concorde Films is useful here.)

One possible way into these photographs is to ask the children which family they would prefer to live in, or to write an imaginative account of how each family might spend its evenings (research in the library would help here). The pupil must include himself as one of the people in the photograph. This will force the children to look *closely* at the differences and likenessess in family make-up – for example, what's it like to go hunting with Dad, when you will die if you don't kill your own food? What's it like to have three mums rather than one, in the Bechuanaland group? What's it like to work as a complete family out in the rice fields? What's it like to go to work with Mum at the age of two, in the Japanese family? How are grandparents valued in the three families on page 27 and the Bechuanaland family? Can you see by the photographs what is the exact position in each family?

*Other Sources*

Contrast accounts of growing up in different parts of the world:
*African Child* by Camara Laye (Fontana).
*Black Boy* by Richard Wright (Longman).
*Tell Freedom* by Peter Abrahams (Faber).
*The Narrow Path* by Francis Selormey (Heinemann African Writers series).
*Twenty Years A-Growing* by Margaret O'Sullivan (Chatto & Windus).
*Long Lance: Autobiography of a Pawnee Chief* (Faber).
*One Small Boy* by Bill Naughton (Panther).
*My Childhood* by Maxim Gorky (Penguin).
*Precocious Autobiography* by Yevgeny Yevtushenko (Penguin).
*The Little World of Foxy* by Norman Smithson (Gollancz).
*Autobiography of a Runaway Slave* by Esteban Montejo (Penguin).
'Reminiscences of Childhood' by Dylan Thomas (*Quite Early One Morning*, Dent) (recorded on Caedmon TC 1132).

One third-year group have produced autobiographies of their own, written and illustrated in a separate booklet form, using file paper, string and cardboard for covers. Inside them, some of them have drawn or painted their own family groups, stuck in relevant pictures from colour supplements, and made cartoons of each member of the family, including the cat and the dog. Then they have taken the finished booklets home, if they wanted to, as a Christmas present. (Another autobiographical form is to get the children to write free verse on each member of the family, with an appropriate drawing or cartoon — see *Meet my Folks* by Ted Hughes (Faber), for an immediate stimulus.)

### 29  Proverb

How many other family proverbs can the group find? Are they always wise sayings? Is this proverb a true comment on the 'spilling soup' passage, for example?

### 30  The Cruel Mother

fillet: a head band for keeping the head-dress in position.

This version is from *The Penguin Book of English Folk Songs* edited by R. Vaughan Williams and A. L. Lloyd.
Contrast the English with the American recorded version on Argo DA 66, 'The Long Harvest' by Ewan MacColl and Peggy Seeger.

### 32–3  Edwardian Family and Victorian Family Groups

I have found the best way to use these photographs is to ask the pupils to bring their own family photograph albums or any loose family snaps, and to see if they can find any photographs as old as these. The discussion starts from these passed round snaps — what was family life like in past ages, for Victorian families, for their grandparents, for their parents? What will it be like in the future? What was Sunday evening like in a house without television fifty or a hundred years ago? Did the man of the house really read a passage from the Bible, while all the women and children listened in silence? Was there hymn singing round the piano? Refer back to the bottom picture on page 32.

(Incidentally, getting the children to write about themselves in fluffy bonnets and sucking dummies is always an absorbing and amusing activity, and usually gives their writing a sharper edge.) 'Having a family or school photograph taken' is another riveting subject, I've found.

#### The Old Photograph Album

The old, dusty, leather-backed album, which was always kept on the top shelf in the cupboard,
Was only produced for visitors and for quiet evenings in winter huddled round a fire.
The faded, yellow photographs neatly set in the thick, black pages must have been fifty years old.
Unknown cousins, aunties, uncles stood outside their houses or in gardens,
in old-fashioned clothes,
Stood like waxwork, with fixed smiles,
Or in the professional photograph the perfectly posed subjects in their best clothes.
Of course mother knew them all, those set faces of the past:
She used to sit with us around her, going through and explaining them all.
Soon we knew them by heart.
But that was years ago and now after all that time,
I have come across that same old album.
The faces are lost, now, though,
but it still brings memories of quiet, winter nights,
And mother long ago.
*Granville Todd (age 13)*

Connection with the history department would of course be invaluable, particularly on the documentary records of family life years ago, for example the contrasted budgets of a family in 1900 and 1914 (what did they spend their money on all those years ago?). These budgets can be found in *Britain in the Modern World* by A. Newth and E. Nash (Penguin). A survey of local church registers and gravestones of local families, and the making of family trees could be very informative.

There is also scope here for outside visits to folk museums, reconstructed houses and streets in social history collections, and, of course, famous houses open to the public. Recently a party from our school, studying the family, visited Abbey House Folk Museum, Kirkstall, Leeds where they were able to make first-hand observations of one of the first wooden mangles (how long did it take Mum to do her washing then?), black-leaded cooking ranges, goffering irons, Victorian fire screens and a whole room of Victorian toys. (How did Jim spend a drizzly Sunday afternoon a hundred years ago?)

*Other Sources*

'Ancestral photograph' by Seamus Heaney (*Death of a Naturalist*, Faber).
*Human Documents of the Industrial Revolution in Britain* by Royston Pike (Allen & Unwin).
*Human Documents of the Victorian Golden Age* by Royston Pike (Allen & Unwin).
*London Labour and the London Poor (1851)* by Henry Mayhew.
Selections by Peter Quennell in *Mayhew's London, Mayhew's Characters* and *London's Underworld* (Spring Books).
Family photograph – *The Railway Game* by Clifford Dyment (page 17) (Dent).

The only way to do justice to one's own area is to hunt through the shelves of the local history section in the nearest library.

### Section Three: The House and the Home (pages 34–5)

The quality of family life is not just made up of the people concerned, it's also affected by the physical condition of the house. So the building itself is worth attention, especially the odd little corners or 'hide-outs' which children take over for themselves or else invest with a special atmosphere. For example the coal cellar where the Bogeyman used to skulk waiting for them to be naughty when they were small, or the cobwebbed attic where Gran's locked trunk still lies in dust, or the frigid best room with its glass cabinet of best crockery never used, all these are powerful themes to write about for children.

For the more practically minded an inventive approach is to design their model home of the future where all the special interests of the family are catered for. (However the design shouldn't be totally far-fetched. It should be kept to reasonable limits.)

*Other sources for the house and the home*

The cellar – *The Four-Storey Mistake* by Elizabeth Enright, pages 32–4 (Puffin).

The playroom — *The Saturdays* by Elizabeth Enright, pages 8–9 (Puffin).
Playing in the attic when wet — *Lark Rise to Candleford* by Flora
Thompson, page 393 (OUP).
At home in a blizzard — *On the Banks of Plum Creek* by Laura Ingalls
Wilder, pages 189–90 (Puffin).
Something found in the attic — *The Owl Service* by Alan Garner, opening
pages (Peacock).
'Sink Song' by J. A. Lindon (*Junior Voices*, 3, Penguin).
'Upstairs' by J. S. Wade (*Junior Voices*, 3, Penguin).
'Up There' and 'Down There' by W. H. Auden (*About the House*, Faber).
(Although there are difficulties in these two poems they are not
insuperable to the thoughtful eleven to thirteen year old.)
'Home Life' by Tom Hastie (Batsford).
'House and Home' edited by M. Barley (Aldis).

**34    Proverb**

Sometimes cleanliness and hygiene become an obsession and children
protest healthily against too much soap too often, or Sunday best for
playing out. See Huck Finn's reaction against Widow Douglas at the
beginning of *Huckleberry Finn* by Mark Twain (Puffin). Jacques Tati's film
*Mon Oncle* (Connoisseur films) makes a superbly funny criticism of family
life in a sterile, plastic house of the future.

**35    The Vacuum**

A testing poem but the mother's fixation with tidiness and house cleaning
is exposed clearly through her death, 'Its bag limp as a stopped lung'. Dirt
has conquered; therefore her preoccupation has been shown to be futile,
in reducing herself to the same level as dirt.

Pupils could perhaps use the idea of personifying a household object — the
vacuum cleaner is referred to as 'sulking, having a mouth, grinning and
howling at filth' — in their writing and cartoon drawings. Some possible
objects might be the spirit of the refrigerator, washing machine, spin-drier,
electric razor, hair dryer, electric toaster, central heating, automatic disposal unit.

*Other Sources*

Housework routine — *The Only Child* by James Kirkup, pages 82–3
(Collins).
Washing day — *Cider with Rosie* by Laurie Lee (Penguin).

Poems
'The Housewife's lament', traditional (*Voices*, 1, Penguin).
'Wash Day', traditional (*Voices*, 1, page 55, Penguin).
'Song of the Old Mother' by W. B. Yeats (*Collected Poems*, Macmillan).

**Section Four: Brothers and Sisters (page 35, see also page 51)**

**35    What a Blessing Younger Brothers Are; Haiku**
*Other Sources*

Brother and sister — *Tom's Midnight Garden* by Philippa Pearce, pages
62–3 (OUP).
'The Magpie' by Alan C. Jenkins (*Springboard*, edited by D. Jackson, Harrap).

'The Button and the Heretic' by David Campbell (*Australian Writing Today*, Penguin).
'The Stone Boy' by Gino Berriault (*Points of View*, Signet).
'Christmas Morning' by Frank O'Connor (*Springboard*, edited by D. Jackson, Harrap).
Looking After a Brother — *Walkabout* by J. V. Marshall, opening chapter (Peacock).

Poems
'The Twins' by H. S. Leigh (*Poetry One: The Key of the Kingdom*, edited by Raymond O'Malley and Denys Thompson, Heinemann).
'The Bramble Briar', traditional (*Penguin Book of English Folk Songs*).
'My Brother Bert' by Ted Hughes (*Meet my Folks*, Faber).
'Nice Brother Martin' by Richard Parker (*Second-hand Family*, BBC pamphlet *Listening and Writing*, Summer 1969).

Photograph
'Looking after a Baby Brother', page 32 (*Springboard*, edited by D. Jackson, Harrap).

## Section Five: Playing Out and Inside, Children's Games (pages 36—48)

The play element is important both within the family and at school; it is here that children relax and expand with all kinds of unseen talents. They flow with words and movement and try on and explore adult family roles, daubing themselves with make-up and teetering round in their Mum's high heels. Why should all this vivacity, imaginative observation and humour be confined to breaks or improvised drama lessons? Why shouldn't textbooks sympathize with and respect children's own idiom and lore?

This area gives wonderful opportunities for a sub-topic — designing adventure playgrounds for families in high-level flats, recording and collection of street games, tape-recording of skipping rhymes and singing games still alive, e.g. 'Old Roger is dead and laid in his grave' (*Junior Voices*, 1, Penguin). 'Spit Nolan' (*Things Working*, page 47).

*Other Sources*

*Children's Games in Street and Playground* by I. and P. Opie (OUP).
*Children's Games* edited by David Holbrook (Gordon Fraser).
'The Key of the Cabinet' by Bill Naughton (*Late Night on Watling Street*, Longman).
Game in the Rain — *Thimble Summer* by Elizabeth Enright (Puffin).
Sliding on the haystacks — *On the Banks of Plum Creek* by Laura Ingalls Wilder, pages 40—45 (Puffin).
'The Wren's Nest' by Liam O'Flaherty (*The Stories of Liam O'Flaherty*, Four Square).
*The Latch-Key Children* by Eric Allen (OUP).
'Boyhood' by Graham Maryon (*Things being Various* edited by L. Stratta, J. Dixon and S. Clements, pages 49—50, OUP).
Street games — *Sons and Lovers* by D. H. Lawrence, page 97 (Penguin).
Children's games — *Lark Rise to Candleford* by Flora Thompson, page 149 (OUP).
I'm the King of the Castle — *King of the Barbareens* by Janet Hitchman, opening pages (Peacock).
Playing section of *Projects* edited by R. Carlen and S. Tottman, pages 82—97 (Macmillan).

Poems
'Chanson Innocente' by E. E. Cummings (*Every Man Will Shout*, OUP).
'Child's Bouncing Song' by Tony Connor (*Voices*, 1, Penguin).
'Boy with Bubble Pipe' by W. Hart-Smith (*The Talking Clothes*, Angus & Robertson).
'Child on Top of a Greenhouse' by Theodore Roethke (*Selected Poems*, Faber; *Voices*, 1, Penguin).
'Birds' Nests' by Edward Thomas (*Collected Poems*, Faber).

Records
*Streets of Song*, Ewan MacColl and Dominic Behan (Topic records, 12T41).
*Children's Singing Games* directed by M. Wilson and J. Gallagher (Topic, Imp A101).
*Deep Lancashire* (Topic, 12T188) (especially 'Hop, Hop, Hop', 'Coalhole Medley' and 'Cob-a-coalin').
*Owdham Edge* (Topic, 12T20) (especially 'Pounds, Shillings and Pence', 'Down at our School' and 'Schoolyard Song').

Photographs
'Hide and Seek in Burslem Churchyard' by Bill Brandt (*Shadow of Light*, Bodley Head).
'Swinging and Playing Football' (*Springboard* edited by D. Jackson, Harrap).
'Dressing Up' (*Things being Various* edited by L. Stratta, S. Clements and J. Dixon, page 85, OUP).
'Tree House', 'Swinging from a Tree', 'Lighting a Bonfire' from *Neill and Summerhill* by John Walmsley (Penguin).

Plays
*St George and the Dragon/Punch and Judy* edited by D. Bell (Puffin).
'The Traditional Play of Punch and Judy' (*Thieves and Angels* edited by David Holbrook, CUP).

## 36  Dressing Up

Interesting in the way the two girls are at the extreme edge of fantasy play — the dangerous, exciting warfare game with the boys is becoming more stimulating than their own dressing up.

## 38, 92  Crazes and Collections

Ask any eleven to thirteen year old child to show you the contents of his pockets and he will probably drag out from the lint a real magpie's nest of random objects. This is what these two pieces of 'Playing out and children's games' are trying to do; to tap children's instincts for hoarding and collecting and to follow up crazes. Even in the layout of the photographs of paper darts, card throwing and bubble blowing and the short prose extracts the impulse of collecting little pieces together into larger wholes has been considered.

A reading of these two pieces (and it might be best to take them together) could lead into interesting collage work. Children could make collections of their own crazes at home and school: conkers, jacks, kites. cap bombs, cotton reel tanks, marbles, card skimming, roller skating, rubber-band cat's cradle, or make lists of their own collections — cheese labels, badges, car and engine numbers, coins, autographs, pressed flowers, football-hero cards – and then design on sugar paper a collage of drawings, free verse, descriptions, instructions to a beginner how to make a cotton-reel tank or play cat's cradle, cuttings from magazines, colour supplements, etc. and then display around the school or classroom.

*Other Sources*

'The Artist' by Shiga Naoya (*Modern Japanese Stories* edited by I. Morris, Eyre & Spottiswoode) (about collecting).
'Feet of Clay' by Brian Glanville (*Goalkeepers are Crazy*, Eyre & Spottiswoode) (autograph hunting).
'Throwing Cigarette Cards' by James Kirkup (*Sorrows, Passions and Alarms*, pages 46–7, Collins).
'Birds' Egg Collecting' by Herbert Read (*Annals of Innocence and Experience*, page 43, Faber).
Rubber bands – *Joby* by Stan Barstow, pages 56–9 (Penguin).
*Something to Do* by Septima (Puffin). (Instructions how to make cotton-reel tanks, page 200; parachute man, pages 192–3; a twizzler, page 238; pipe-cleaner men, pages 210–11; finger shadows, page 34.)

**43–6  Door Knocking**

See *Lore and Language of School-Children* by I. and P. Opie, page 377, 'Pranks' (OUP).
Here the Opies give more than sixty established names for 'the pursuit of illegally knocking at doors'; and some lively descriptions: other lawless children's games, such as 'Mischief Night: 4 November in the North of England' (pages 276–80) or 'Guy Fawkes Day' (pages 280–83).

An evocative discussion point is why did the children run away from Mrs Jaffer, and yet love tormenting the other grown-ups?

**47  Serious Games**

Children write sincerely on the theme of games which started out as games but ended up bitterly. Can you ever have a 'friendly fight' without hurting anyone?

*Other Sources*

Funeral game – *Grandad with Snails* by Michael Baldwin (Hutchinson).
'Glory of the Moon' by Joyce Cary (*Spring Song and Other Stories*, Penguin).

**48  People**

There are always moments of loneliness in playing out or at break when a child feels an outsider, sneered at by the group, or teachers, or by parents or by best friends.

Children could try their hand at concrete poems to express a similar sense of isolation in a crowd. Cutting out heads or rows of people and then pasting them on to a piece of drawing paper might be a stimulus to this kind of experiment.

**Section Six: Family Sayings (page 49)**

Several talented first formers produced some bold cartoons illustrating some of these sayings, such as, 'You've got carrots growing out of your ears', 'Tied to his mother's apron strings' or 'My how you've grown'.

You've got carrotts growing out of your ears

MY HOW YOU'VE GROWN

*Craig Judge, Alan Wild and Glen Fallows: Aged 11, Whitworth High School*

TIED TO HIS MOTHER'S APRON
STRINGS

MY, HOW YOU'VE GROWN

I'VE GOT TO MUCH ON MY PLATE

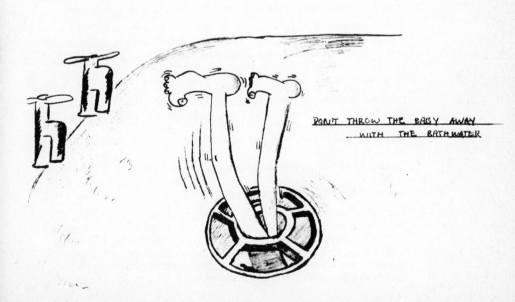

DON'T THROW THE BABY AWAY WITH THE BATHWATER

Other ways of using this list are to use them as starting points for group improvised drama, e.g. a visit from an aunt and uncle who have been abroad for three years, using, 'My, how you've grown!' or a play about a boy who pretended to be sweet natured and innocent when in sight of his parents but was by himself a real tearaway, using, 'Butter wouldn't melt in his mouth'.

Another possibility is to make a list of family sayings for your own group or for the whole school. You might start by pinning this list on the wall and asking for any other interesting family phrases.

### Section Seven: Relationships Between Boys and Girls (pages 50—52)

A very delicate subject and needs handling with great sympathy and tact. At this age group we're not aiming at the full emotional engagement of the fourteen to sixteen year old, but the shy, curious skirmishings of the eleven to thirteen year old at home and school that we found in 'Dressing Up' (page 36) and 'Are the lads watching us?' interest in the opposite sex.

In 'Where Do Babies Come From' the humorous tone saves the piece from becoming an adolescent awkwardness. Talking points sprout everywhere, e.g. what does the Father mean by his use of the word 'natural' in line eight? Do the boy's mother and Miss Cooney treat him in a way which will encourage the boy to have a healthy attitude to sex? How will the pupils answer their own children's questions? By making up stories about 'birds and flowers', 'gooseberry bushes', 'storks'? (Cartoons here on parents' evasions of the subject?)

**51, 52    Banter, Bickering**

These extracts show that an early interest is often expressed through verbal battles, repartee, teasing, even through open aggression as a cover up for embarrassment, as in the Peanuts cartoon on page 53.

Some of this verbal one-upmanship and revelling in 'argufying' should be caught, either in writing or tape-recording or just talking in groups.

'Bickering' gives a useful stimulus to this kind of work, with Sid's ingeniously literal response to 'Say you're sorry'. Improvisation could come in here on misunderstandings between boys and girls.

*Other Sources*

Engaged to Becky — *Tom Sawyer* by Mark Twain (Dent).
Meeting a girl — *The Beautiful Years* by Henry Williamson, pages 108—10 (Faber).
Children's questions — *King of the Barbareens* by Janet Hitchman, pages 54—5 (Peacock).
Scaring a girl — *Grandad with Snails* by Michael Baldwin (Hutchinson).

### Section Eight: Leaving Home (pages 54—6)

The disturbance of moving house usually forces us to assess what that particular aura of home has meant to us. An outside visit to a house about to be demolished can help enormously to get the children to respond specifically — 'the iodine stain on the baseboard, Randy's pictures, plasticine marks on the office ceiling, the height-measuring marks of each Melendy child on the upstairs bathroom door' — to the special atmosphere of a deserted house, or what particularly a home has meant to them for several years.

Improvisation can help children to empathize for that sense of rootlessness and loss connected with moving house or eviction, e.g. careless removal men thumping around possessions that are precious to you, or an argument between council men and an old couple about having to move from a house they've lived in for fifty years, or a family who love pets having to move to high-level flats where pets are not allowed. Tape-recorded interviews with families about to move are an invaluable help if the group listens to these before improvising.

For a change of approach a fruitful comic situation is that where removal men have to move a priceless grand piano through a narrow doorway with disastrous results!

*Other Sources*

Eviction — *Bonnie Pit Laddie* by Frederick Grice, page 84 (OUP).
Moving house — *Little House on the Prairie* by Laura Ingalls Wilder, page 8 (Puffin).
Moving in — *Little House on the Prairie* by Laura Ingalls Wilder, page 52.

Poems
'A New House' by Edward Thomas (*Collected Poems,* Faber).
'House Moving' by Patricia Hubbell (*Junior Voices,* 1, Penguin).
'The Chant of the Awakening Bulldozers' by Patricia Hubbell (*Junior Voices,* 1, Penguin).
'The Little Cart' by Ch'en Tsu Lung (*Voices,* 1, Penguin).

This subject might be rewardingly extended to include the homeless family, or drop out (see *Positives* by Ander and Thom Gunn, pages 74—7, Faber, especially the pictures). For leaflets, display posters and information, Shelter will supply these willingly (86 The Strand, London, WC2). An exhibition on homeless families might be mounted in the school and some form of contribution made towards Shelter.

Photographs
Pages 5 and 44 of *Junior Voices,* 1; page 46 of *Junior Voices,* 3; page 29 of *Junior Voices,* 4 (Penguin).

56   **Evacuated**

This extract appears in *The Evacuees* edited by B. S. Johnson (Gollancz). There are many other moving descriptions of being separated from the family and treated like a stranger in another part of Britain. See especially Christopher Leach's and B. S. Johnson's contributions to the book.

**Section Nine: Family Illness (pages 57—60)**

57   **Pretending to be Ill on Monday Morning**

This is a richly comic and human situation to improvise upon in group dramatic work.

*Other Sources*

'The Use of Force' by William Carlos Williams (*Points of View,* Signet).
Fever dream — *Cider with Rosie* by Laurie Lee (Penguin).

Fever in the family — *Little House on the Prairie* by Laura Ingalls Wilder (Puffin).
Seeing one's mother in hospital — *Joby* by Stan Barstow, pages 77–8 (Penguin).
'Malade' by D. H. Lawrence (*Complete Poems*, Heinemann).
'Boy with Cancer' by David Wevill (*Penguin Modern Poets*, 4).

**60    I've gota Code id by Doze**

Perhaps the pupils could be encouraged to play with language in a similar attempt to reproduce the exact sounds made by other illnesses and difficulties, e.g. a person with a sore throat, gargling, or a person who keeps losing his voice, or a person with hiccoughs.

**Section Ten: Death in the Family (page 61)**

**61    Ritual**

*Other Sources*

Death in the family — *This Time Next Week*, by Leslie Thomas, page 29 (Blackie).
Diaries are generally very helpful for this topic, providing many domestic episodes and special occasions in the family. For example:
The funeral — *Kilvert's Diary* by Francis Kilvert, pages 93–5 (Cape).
A country funeral — *Journals of Dorothy Wordsworth* by Dorothy Wordsworth, edited by Helen Darbishire, pages 51–2, 3 September 1800 (OUP).

Poems
'Mid-Term Break' by Seamus Heaney (*Death of a Naturalist*, Faber).
'In Memory of Jane Fraser' by Geoffrey Hill (*The New Poetry* edited by A. Alvarez, Penguin).
'The Lesson' by Edward Lucie-Smith (*Penguin Modern Poets*, 6).
'Spring and Fall' by Gerard Manley Hopkins (*The Poems of Gerard Manley Hopkins*, Penguin).
'Bells for John Whiteside's Daughter' by John Crowe Ransom (*Iron, Honey, Gold*, vol. 2, edited by David Holbrook, CUP).

**Section Eleven: Starting School (pages 62–3)**

**62–3    Taking the Register**

This extract is taken from *Albert Angelo* by B. S. Johnson (Panther). Could children 'register' their own class group in words and pictures — character sketches and a portrait gallery of the whole form?

An interesting aspect of this passage is the way the inner thoughts of the teacher are put in, in italics. There's scope here for getting the children to look at themselves through the eyes of a teacher — inner thoughts of a history teacher first period Monday morning. The result *should* be a more sympathetic form!

*Other Sources*

A country journey — *Springfield Home* by E. Stucley, pages 9–13 (Puffin).
Paper round and being late for school — *A Severnside Story* by Frederick Grice, pages 29–30 (OUP).

An African journey to school — *The Narrow Path* by Francis Selormey,
pages 128–30 (Heinemann African Writers series).
Meeting a stranger on a journey to school — *The Summer Birds* by
Penelope Farmer, opening pages (Chatto & Windus).
Paper round and results in school — *Gumble's Yard* by John Rowe
Townsend, pages 75–6 (Puffin).

Poems
'Bus to School' by John Walsh (*Roundabout by the Sea*, Heinemann).
'Schoolboy' by W. Hart-Smith (*The Talking Clothes*, Angus & Robertson).
'Schoolboys in Winter' by John Clare (*Selected Poems of John Clare* edited
by James Reeves, Heinemann).

**64–5   First Day at School**

Dear Miss,
Two years ago, when I was in first magistrale [a four-year upper school leading to a
diploma for elementary school teachers] you used to make me feel shy.

As a matter of fact, shyness has been with me all my life. As a little boy I used to
keep my eyes on the ground. I would creep along the walls in order not to be seen.

(*Letter to a Teacher* by the School of Barbiana, page 17, Penguin).

We, the safe adults, tend to forget the 'paralysing shyness' of a first day in
a new school, especially for timid children. Tape-recorded interviews of
various 'first days' would sharpen discussion here — how can schools, and
teachers in particular, help children like Richard to get over their
nervousness and isolation? How could the children in this extract have
helped Richard?

One positive way of helping, and usually providing a most absorbing
lesson, is to ask all the second and third formers to write a letter of advice
to first formers to be kept by the teacher and handed to the new children
on their first day. For example, here's some advice from a second former:

Try to keep out of fights. If you do fight and have to go to the headmaster it gets
you a bad name all through the school.

If you want to keep some friends in the class don't tell tales of anyone unless you
have to or unless everyone wants you to.

Try not to start bawling about little things like getting an easy question wrong or
you will be known as Softy.

*John Lund (age 12)*

*Other Sources*

The first day of school — *Little Children* by William Saroyan (Faber).
Billy the kid — *The Hot Gates* by William Golding (Faber).
First day — *Cider with Rosie* by Laurie Lee, page 43 (Penguin).
First day — *Village School* by Miss Read, pages 22, 42–3 (Penguin).
New Teacher — *The Narrow Path* by Francis Selormey (Heinemann African
Writers series).
An interesting reversed viewpoint, of a young teacher anxious about facing
children is to be found in *These Happy Golden Years* by Laura Ingalls
Wilder, chapter two onwards (Puffin).
Initiation ceremonies — *Lore and Language of School Children* by I. and P.
Opie, pages 292–3 (OUP).

The aim here, by presenting contrasted children's attitudes, is to provoke a fair assessment of and positive reaction to school assemblies. If children find fault with their assembly (realizing, of course, that the 1944 Education Act made school assemblies compulsory) what changes would they like to see made and why. If the school is liberal enough perhaps they will have the opportunity of putting something on for assembly, e.g. prepare a modern, improvised drama version of one of the Bible stories and perform it. Write a story or a free-verse poem which you think suitable to be read out in assembly. Make a collection of poems, stories, plays, songs that you think would make an impact in assembly, etc.

*Other Sources*

Assembly — *The Humpy in the Hills* by John Gunn, pages 13–17 (Puffin). *The Cambridge Hymnal* edited by David Holbrook and E. Poston (CUP). A programme about childhood selected by David Holbrook, *Thieves and Angels*, pages 157–67 (CUP). (A stimulus for the children's own collections and a choice of material that implies that assemblies should be celebrations of life in the widest sense.)
Children's views on assembly — *The School that I'd Like* edited by Edward Blishen, pages 107–12 (Penguin).

**Section Twelve: The School Day (pages 68–71)**

**68–71**    **Keeping a Diary**

Royston Lambert's *The Hothouse Society* (Weidenfeld & Nicolson), from which all these extracts are taken, is a valuable help in presenting many truthful accounts of boarding school life.

The effort of trying to record one's own school routine in a diary is always worthwhile, but the children must be encouraged to observe honestly and precisely and to use their senses freshly in these daily entries. Without this encouragement, banal, flat statements are usually the result.

Group discussion is usually sparked off by some of the extracts and pictures in this theme — a public-school *v.* state-school debate can start from the photographs on pages 68–9; a boarding-school *v.* day-school debate can arise from the starkness of the dormitory scene on page 71.

Some of the social attitudes and values need very careful probing, especially the entry on page 71, the prayer by a boy at a prep school.

*Other Sources*

*Portrait of the Artist as a Young Man* by James Joyce (Penguin). B B C TV documentary on Eton.

**Section Thirteen: Break and Dinner Activities (pages 72–6)**

The playground is the place where children can relax and be themselves away from the necessity to please the teacher (for general comments and suggestions on children's games and the play element, see Section Five, pages 36–48) but it can also be a brutal and challenging place where they have to prove themselves against the giggles and sneers (see especially 'True, Dare, Love, Kiss, Lick or Promise and Fight').

## 72    Kiss Chase

'Petticoat Thursday' and 'Kissing Friday': according to a custom current at Settle High, Yorkshire (1967), all boys are allowed special permission for one day to pull girls' petticoats and snatch a kiss.

Children's memories and tales about their primary schools are still clear in their mind at this age group, and they usually tell or write about these episodes with great relish and gusto.

## 72    Rhythm

The non-academic child, who finds a physical dignity in out-of-the-classroom activities, is very common. Jerry's top of the head 'rhythm' means nothing to the boy narrator, but he finds the true meaning of the word in his own graceful and exuberant movement, seen in the last eight lines of the poem.

How far do the tone of voice, syntax and deliberate mis-spelling help the poem?
Line 10 — 'Law': is there a topical pun here, referring to Denis Law the Manchester United and Scotland forward, and to an intuitive control?

*Other Sources*

Games lesson — *A Kestrel for a Knave* by Barry Hines, pages 86—108 (Penguin).
Poetry and football — *A Precocious Autobiography* by Yevgeny Yevtushenko, page 60 (Penguin).
House football — *The Beautiful Years* by Henry Williamson, pages 189—90 (Faber).
School sport — *This Time Next Week* by Leslie Thomas, pages 56—8 (Blackie).
Sports-day — *Village School* by Miss Read, page 223 (Penguin).
Accident in the gym — *To Sir, with Love* by E. R. Brathwaite, page 114 (Four Square).
All kids are equal — *The School that I'd Like* edited by Edward Blishen, pages 79—82 (Penguin).

Poems
'Prayer of a Black Boy' by Guy Tirolien (*This Day and Age*, Edward Arnold).
'The Airy Tomb' by R. S. Thomas (*Song at the Year's Turning*, Hart-Davis).

## 73    True, Dare, Love, Kiss, Lick or Promise

Compare other 'dare' situations in:
The dare to see Boo Radley — *To Kill a Mockingbird* by Harper Lee, pages 19—21 (Penguin).
'Duffings' by E. W. Hildick (*In a Few Words* edited by Alfred Bradley, Edward Arnold).

Plays
*Julian* by Ray Jenkins (BBC *Listening and Writing* pamphlet, Autumn 1970).
*Chicken* by Gordon Lyall (BBC *Listening and Writing* pamphlet, Spring 1970).
*The Chicken Run* by Aidan Chambers (Heinemann).

Notice the way fear alternates with a feeling of self-importance in the boy's reactions to the fight, until physical pain eventually breaks down the Hollywood posturing and he suddenly realizes the truth about himself.

An interesting class survey could start from the descriptions of the mysteriously large circle of strangers urging on the fight, e.g. try to find out whether the rest of the class tries to stop fights in the playground, or whether they egg the fighters on and shout for blood. (Sensible reasons for opinions expressed are needed here.)

*Other Sources*

Fight with the stranger — *Tom Sawyer* by Mark Twain, pages 6—9 (Dent).
The fight — *Portrait of the Artist as a Young Dog* by Dylan Thomas (Dent).
Fight with a bully — *A Kestrel for a Knave* by Barry Hines, pages 75—8 (Penguin).
*Sprightly Running* by John Wain (Macmillan) (many examples of being victimized).
*Joby* by Stan Barstow, pages 68—9 (Penguin) (see 'Telling Tales' by Camara Laye, page 114).

Collections of children's use of a language of intimidation might start from 'Have you made your will out yet?' or 'Has he got his coffin with him?' (See *Lore and Language of School Children* by I. and P. Opie, page 195, 'Fighting' pages 196—8, OUP.)

## Section Fourteen: The Classroom, Buildings and Lessons

**78    Discovery**

Too much of the writing about school tends to present the teachers as harsh dictators (look at the stereotyped fossils still appearing in children's comics), and school as a dreary routine. So in this extract I have attempted to redress the balance — that school can be a relaxed, friendly and often stimulating place and the teachers sympathetic.

As the discovery method of teaching gains ground in more schools and more subjects, many more children will experience the excitement of finding out something about themselves or the world they live in, instead of being given experiments to prove. This extract could lead on to descriptions of discoveries in science (using the picture on page 79 — 'What does happen when it boils?'), discoveries through a microscope in biology, discoveries in a pond or at the sea-shore, self-discovery in drama or in the gym.

*Other Sources*

History lesson — *A Severnside Story* by Frederick Grice, pages 32—3 (OUP).

Cartoons
'Good Morning Richard!' — *A Hundred of the Best* edited by Nicholas Tucker, page 80 (Penguin).
'A Question of Faith' by Vernon Scannell (*Mastering the Craft*, Pergamon Poets).

Lower School
Most lessons in open-plan 'home base'
unit of 120 children.
No streaming by ability or rigid divisions
between subjects.

Upper School
Also open plan but more lecture halls
and specialist areas, e.g. science labs.
Carpeted 'Common room' for older
students.

Resources Area
Assembly hall, P.E., music and staff
rooms.
Also cafeteria and library with extensive
audio-visual equipment.

Community Area
Facilities for further education,
e.g. evening classes and youth clubs.
Ideally a general community and sporting
centre.

Photographs

Clay modelling, woodwork, needlework — *Neill and Summerhill* by John Walmsley (Penguin).

## 78    Classroom of the 1930s

'The very sight of the old, red-bricked school, with tiled walls and big, ugly blackboards, could never inspire anyone to learn' (page 45 of *The School that I'd Like* edited by Edward Blishen, Penguin). Children are very inventive in designing their perfect schools, or schools of the future. Involved in this fantasy extension is a very real awareness of what is lacking in atmosphere and building in most of our schools.

This project could start from the atmosphere of your own school — is it any different from James Kirkup's 'Classroom of the 1930s'. A detailed recording of the atmosphere in most rooms of the school could lead into plans for model classrooms and then a whole school, or instead of plans, written explanations.

A different approach is to link up with the history department and find out what the material conditions of schools were like in the past (see *Learning and Teaching in Victorian Times* (Longman 'Then and There' series), and the pictures in *Education* edited by Malcolm Seaborne, Visual History of Britain, Aldus) or find out something about the differences in school buildings in different parts of the country. (See contrasting pictures in *Half our Future*, HMSO between pages 108 and 109, and perhaps show a plan of the latest in school buildings, e.g. Valley Winds School in St Louis, Missouri or Countesthorpe College in Leicestershire, see the previous page.)

*Other Sources*

School, 2000 A D and Dark relics that our age is afraid to demolish — *The School that I'd Like* edited by E. Blishen, pages 31 and 44–5 (Penguin). Pictures of classrooms — *Neill and Summerhill* by John Walmsley (Penguin).

**Section Fifteen: Homework (pages 78–91)**

## 78    Haiku

Haiku writing, usually three lines of five, seven, five syllables, but can vary either side of this number of syllables, teaches children the importance of simplicity and economy in their own writing (see *The Penguin Book of Japanese Verse* translated by G. Bownas and A. Thwaite).

## 82    Running Away

'How did school go then?'
'Oh, o.k., Dad.'

Children find it so difficult to convey the actual demands of school honestly to worried parents that they usually give up and hide behind banalities. How could Paul explain to his parents that genuine understanding of his maths problems was secondary to his fear of being caned for not having finished his homework?

Most children I have read this story to understand intuitively the reasons for Paul's truanting and respond to the peculiar sense of hollowness that prevents Paul from enjoying his temporary escape from his problem.

Preliminary discussion and perhaps writing about their own inability to do homework, or days when they have truanted, or other situations from their own experience that show 'How treacherous adults were!' might help children to involve themselves in the story.

Question 19 of the 'Home and School' Questionnaire, page 109, might be worthwhile following up here into a class survey.

*Other Sources*

Collecting the homework – *Dandelion Days* by Henry Williamson, pages 131–2 (Faber).
*The School that I'd Like* edited by Edward Blishen, page 74 (Penguin).

## Section Sixteen: Swopping and Collecting (page 92)

### 92 Collections

For this piece and the photographs on page 94–5, see page 38 and pages 46 and 47 of the Handbook.

## Section Seventeen: School Punishment (pages 96–9)

### 96–9 Punishment

I have found the best way of introducing the 'Spare the rod/spoil the child' problem is to get the pupils to talk into the situation by expressing how they use power when *they* are in a position of authority, e.g. how do they train a spoilt puppy or get a young child to do what they ask? Or how do they behave as Form monitors, or representatives, or Captain of a school team? (see 'Being Form Captain' in 'Writing about Experiences' by J. H. Walsh in *Teaching English*, Heinemann). In what situation have they hit an animal or person, and did the blow have the required effect?

Then one could discuss Mr Gubb's actions from a more thoughtful position – was Mr Gubb right to use the cane in this situation? Why do you think he uses the cane with such force? Should the cane ever be given as a result of personal anger, or is this the only time to give it? Why didn't the second boy himself tell Mr Gubb of his septic hand? Do you think the second boy is soft when he starts to cry? What would you have done in Mr Gubb's position? Bearing this extract in mind discuss, 'A good thrashing did nobody any harm. I had to go through it myself and it was the making of me.'

*Other Sources*

Prefect uses a pandybat – *Portrait of the Artist as a Young Man* by James Joyce (Penguin).
Being thrashed in assembly – *Bonnie Pit Laddie* by Frederick Grice, pages 61–4 (OUP).
Beating – *Grandad with Snails* by Michael Baldwin, page 74 (Hutchinson).
Disciplining Fletcher – *No More School* by William Mayne, pages 92–102 (Puffin).
'Noulded into a shake' by Patrick Campbell (*Springboard* edited by D. Jackson, Harrap).

Poem
'Brainy teacher is it you . . .' – *Medieval English Verse* translated by Brian Stone, page 106 (Penguin).

Record
*Children Talking:* Music for Pleasure (EMI MFP1224).
(Getting into trouble — where a Burnley schoolboy tells of why he was expelled from school.)

Cartoon
'The Mark of Cane' — *A Hundred of the Best* edited by Nicholas Tucker (Penguin).

Photograph
A fight — *Violence* by Colin Ward, page 33 (Penguin).

### Section Eighteen: Examinations (pages 100–103)

Children need to remind themselves of their own individuality, 'I am me', in a system that reduces them very often to the level of drab uniformity, or of 'candidates'. The juxtaposition of the photographs on page 100 and 101, and page 100 and 102 (that regimented regularity of desks is no accident!) could be used to introduce discussion on this subject, e.g. do most schools need to be so competitive? — look at those cups acting as visible lures just above the 'Examination' notice in the photograph on page 101.

The tense, rustling atmosphere of the examination room, and desk lid tops offer great scope for free-verse writing.

**101  Examination**

poss sticks: used for pounding clothes clean in water.

*Other Sources*

'This Almighty God' — *The School that I'd Like* edited by Edward Blishen, pages 113–24 (Penguin).

Cartoons
*A Hundred of the Best* edited by Nicholas Tucker, pages 52–3 (Penguin).

### Section Nineteen: School Food (pages 104–6)

As a corrective to the typical 'Ugh!' unthinking reaction of so many children to school dinners it might be a good idea to get the pupils to find out how much money is at the school cook's disposal (and what other regulations she has to comply with, e.g. vitamin content, etc.) and then ask them to draw up a week's menu for the whole school, keeping within the budget.

I have found that children get very concerned when they are considering whether it's good sense to force a child to eat something up: 'Now you're just going to sit there till you finish it, if it takes you all night.' Will the pupils ask the same of their own children, when they have spent the whole morning preparing food?

**106  School Language**

Is there such a thing as a school language, used specifically for school activities? Could the children make their own collections within their own school and perhaps find out how local some of this language is by writing to friends in other schools in other parts of the country? (Perhaps the teacher could fix up some kind of form exchange?)

*Other Sources*

School dinners – *Lore and Language of School Children* by I. and P. Opie (OUP).
'I won't eat the fish' episode – the plays *My Flesh, My Blood* or *Spring and Port Wine* by Bill Naughton (French).
'One of the main grumbles' – *The School that I'd Like* edited by Edward Blishen (Penguin).

Photograph
Contrast photographs of Summerhill school dinners in *Neill and Summerhill* by John Walmsley (Penguin), with the photograph on page 105.


## Section Twenty: The Medical Side of School (page 107)

**107    An Injection**

Children usually write very well about their own anxiety caused by visits to the school dentist, doctor, nurse, optician. Also the presence of strangers around school makes them observe their own classroom atmosphere more closely (see 'Glasses', *Things Working*, page 45).

*Other Sources*

Visit to the optician – *Grandad with Snails* by Michael Baldwin (Hutchinson).
Medical at school – *Sorrows, Passions and Alarms* by James Kirkup, page 84 (Collins).
Heart condition? – *A London Childhood* by John Holloway, pages 15–16, 24 (Routledge & Kegan Paul).
School inspector – *Lark Rise to Candleford* by Flora Thompson, page 202 (OUP).

Poem
'With Half an Eye' by Philip Hobsbaum (*Happenings* edited by D. Grugeon, Harrap).


## Section Twenty-One: Home and School Questionnaire (pages 108–9)

**108–9    Home and School Questionnaire**

This questionnaire is not intended to be used only once. Its real purpose is to stimulate all kinds of different activities: the questions can be simply taken as discussion points for small-group work. (The class divides into groups of four or five, who then elect their own leader and choose their own topic for discussion from the list. The leader takes notes on the group's views and reports back to the whole class group and the teacher.) Or class-group work: a class survey is started on one question and bar graphs are made from the information obtained. Or one person fills in the questionnaire and conclusions are drawn by the questioner; the questions are used for tape-recording topics and the results are played back to the whole group and discussed.

**Section Twenty-Two: Playing Truant**

See notes on 'Running Away' (page 82).

**112—13   Visit to the Headmaster**

Write on being called out in front of the whole class, or thoughts on waiting outside the Head's study.

*Other Sources*

Film
*Kes,* Kenneth Loach and Tony Garnett (United Artists).
(The episode where the 'Smoker's Union' are waiting for the Head outside his study and plant all their cigarettes on an innocent first-year boy.)

The circus — *My Name is Aram* by William Saroyan (Faber).
Noah's Ark — *The Loneliness of the Long-Distance Runner* by Alan Sillitoe (Pan).

**Section Twenty-Three: Splitting: An Exploration of the School Child's Code of Honour (pages 113—19)**

As a contrast to the shortness of some of the sections, this theme has been explored more lengthily from several different angles.

Children fear the unpopularity of the 'sneak' or 'tell-tale' label and often hide behind a class loyalty to the code of not splitting, but when discussing 'telling tales' most children see that in cases of extreme victimization, splitting becomes a fair, responsible action.

**113   Owning Up**

'Owning up' shows us a teacher's exploitation of 'a sense of honour' and perhaps makes us more sympathetic towards the person who doesn't own up but hides in the anonymity of the group in a tensely silent room when the teacher demands to know, 'Who did it?'

**118—19   School Thief**

'School thief' introduces the roles of the school scapegoat (Georgie Pringle) and the teacher's pet (Nigel Barton). Here we have a further extension of the theme; the 'tell-tale' who is astute enough to use the prejudice of the teacher to save his own skin. Miss Tilling's witch-hunt methods of gaining the evidence she needs from Bert are worth discussing.

Work could start from this idea of approaching a single topic from several angles, e.g. Write about a situation where someone in the desk behind sticks a pin in a boy, but this boy is caught by the teacher retaliating, and is given some lines: (a) The person who used the pin. (Is he going to own up and take the blame?) (b) The boy who was caught by the teacher. (Should he split on the person behind him?) (c) The teacher's angle. (Should he listen to the complaints of B and spend time on finding out the truth of the incident?) (d) An onlooker from the rest of the class. (Does he get involved by trying to help?)

*Other Sources*

TV play
*Why Danny misses school* by Keith Dewhurst (shown in the 1969 B B C schools programme, Easter term). An experiment in a multi-viewpoint play. The same events seen through the eyes of four different people with suitable distortion to reflect character. The viewer has to judge the truth.

*Stand up Nigel Barton* by Dennis Potter, B B C TV (Clips from the original Wednesday play would help this extract.)
Should Joby split on Gus Wilson? – *Joby* by Stan Barstow, pages 57–60 (Penguin).
The schoolboy code of honour – *An Only Child* by Frank O'Connor, pages 118–20 (Macmillan).

## Section Twenty-Four: The End of School (page 120)

The deserted atmosphere of an empty school is extremely potent (the contrast with the daytime noise and confusion reinforces this power I suppose) and children respond immediately to it.

Write on 'Alone in school buildings at night' or 'The end of school to a cleaner or caretaker' or 'The end of term'.

*Other Sources*

Last day of term – *Going to the Moon* by Philip Callow, pages 55–61 (MacGibbon & Kee).

Poems
'School's Out' by Hal Summers (*Echoes of Experience*, Longman).
'School's Out' by W. H. Davies (*Collected Poems*, Faber).
'The Place's Fault' by Philip Hobsbaum (*The Place's Fault*, Macmillan).
'Last Lesson of the Afternoon' by D. H. Lawrence (*Complete Poems*, Heinemann).

# Things Working
## Penny Blackie

The material in this book is concerned with things working. My concern is with the way children work. The selection attempts to harness and feed both a recognized and a latent fascination with the things and people that work around us. In many ways the processes that are described in the bulk of the pieces echo some of the processes of learning in which children are involved. Through the material in *Things Working* I hope children will be encouraged to take a fresh look at the world around them, to re-examine, to question, even to re-create.

The way that this theme impinges on children's lives is in one sense actual, physical and concrete, and in another sense overt and abstract, dealing with ideas and notions and fantasies. This open-ended quality has had advantages and drawbacks. It made possible the inclusion of a wide variety of items, but in so doing ran the risk of making the choice so wide, so ambivalent that it made the topic disparate and incoherent.

It was necessary, therefore, to apply some limiting factors and a very loose structure has been imposed: as an introduction to the topic, pages 9–13 deal with the sometimes strange and always very personal way of looking at things; pages 41–64 present, in varying ways, the machines about us, those that affect our everyday lives; pages 65–83 form a section on industrial archaeology; pages 84–98 are concerned with people working and pages 100–120 are largely about the future.

Historically, education in this country has been an additive process — teachers cram in as much information as the child can take. With the advances made in this century, the store of knowledge has become so great that teachers have had to re-think their aims for education. Many teachers are now beginning to say that what has to happen in schools is learning, not teaching, and that this must happen through helping children to think rather than by imparting knowledge.

The selection in *Things Working* aims at helping children to think in a variety of ways. The zany creative thinking of Heath Robinson's marvellous inventions will strike a chord in the imagination of many children, most of whom still have the ability to challenge conventions and assumptions about the way things should work. In a slightly extended way this can develop into genuine inventiveness — instead of creating a joke, to create a machine that really will do a job better and in a way which people have never thought of before ('A Machine for Travelling over Rough Ground', page 29). However, there is also a place for the artistic creation that uses known techniques, ranging from the first throes of discovery ('Plastecine Sculpture', page 18) to the experience of Sandburg's potter ('Jug', page 25) and eventually the masterly, sophisticated inventions and creations of Leonardo da Vinci (page 27) and Brunel (pages 66–70).

I see the fostering and valuing of such creative thinking as an important way of working with this book. Any kind of creative achievement (whether actual or conceptual) involves a very special use of time, care, thought and loving attention, and the sense of completeness when this stage is reached is an experience all children should be entitled to. To achieve this will depend on an atmosphere in the classroom that enables children to follow up, individually or in small groups, particular interests and ideas suggested by the material. I do not expect all children to like or be stimulated by all of the pieces: I would hope that there were no children who were not excited by some of them. I should be pleased to see the sort of flexibility in the classroom which would allow one group of children to work for half a term on designing and building something, or on a radio ballad, while another group might get bored with the topic and move away onto another theme.

I would also hope that a wide variety of activities would take place. The children in our secondary schools do an enormous amount of writing — far more than is really necessary for their learning. This has far-reaching side effects and perhaps I could quote an example of how it affects learning.

I am working on the Nuffield *Resources for Learning* Project with a class of third-year girls. The work is all of the type I have described, individual or group work based on themes with a wide selection of materials available. The first unit took three weeks and in that time all the girls produced a prodigious amount of work of all kinds. However, those girls who spent most of their time on non-writing activities (tape-recording, acting, talking, reading, making things) ended up feeling guilty that they had not produced as much writing as their friends and felt that they had not been working. It is a horrifying indictment of their seven years of education that two formulae emerged: work equals writing; and anything that is enjoyed cannot be work.

For the children using *Things Working*, I sincerely hope that writing will form only a part of their activities and that they will also be talking, reading, making tapes, collages, paintings, wall posters, drawing comic strips, inventing and designing, acting and so on. However, this is not to decry the importance of writing and I should particularly like to stress one approach to writing — the need to look very closely at what you are writing about in order to gain a sense of the total experience. In her description of Laura's Pa making a door, Laura Ingalls Wilder does this (page 38) as does Ian Griffiths in 'Carving a Goldfish' (page 24). It may be a description of what something looks like or it may be the careful relating of a process — either way, it affords the child a very close and reflective way of looking at things that I feel is vital to the use of language.

One of the best ways of handling this is through direct experience. I have a couple of lessons a week in the Art Room with a class of eleven year olds, where there is a display table of various objects. The children had all *seen* the objects several times but had not *looked* at them. One day I asked them to choose one of those things, to look at it very closely in a small group and talk about what it was like. If they wanted to write about it, that was fine. One group talked about a dried artichoke and Julia wrote about it.

## The Artichoke

I think that this odd flower looks like a poor face reaching up to the sun. It has a sort of pin-cushion with feathers around it. I think that it is funny for it looks like a hairbrush or a back scrubber.

It also looks as if it is dead and withered. The Artichoke is a dirty looking flower and I feel sorry for this poor, feathered, hairbrush, withered flower.

*(Julia Witt)*

In these five sentences different things are happening. In the second and third sentences she has been fairly strongly influenced by the talk in her group and there is no involvement in what she says. Somehow, by starting a new paragraph she shakes herself clear of the others and says what *she* wanted to say, which is what she hesitantly started saying at the beginning. I don't think Julia could have written this if she had not had the artichoke there, and possibly if she had not discussed it with her friends. I feel that this is a valuable activity, it is part of the life around her and in her own way Julia is coming to terms with it. There are poems in *Things Working* that could possibly operate as this sort of starting-point ('Glasses', page 45, 'A View of Things', page 13) but far better to use the life the children live.

(One could also, in passing, use this example to answer a criticism that has been put to me about anthologies that contain pictures; namely, that the freshness of impact is lost if the children have an opportunity to flick through or browse through the book. The freshness of an *immediate* impact may admittedly be lost, but the value of a very precise, very reflective, very conscious look at a picture (or any other visual stimulus) does at least in part compensate for this.)

When we consider the life children live in the context of a theme like *Things Working*, it is temptingly easy to see the destructive side of technology and progress — the soullessness, the human sacrifice. There have been 8000 generations of man and in the last generation alone more has happened in science and technology than ever before. That this is changing our lives cannot be denied. Yet, what also cannot be denied is our refusal to face up to it, to adjust our lives accordingly. When asked about the changes they think they will see in their own generation, children are not lacking in ideas — they talk about holidays on the moon, new inventions and gadgets — but they fail to see any of these changes as directly affecting their own lives. They will still grow up, marry, work, live in houses, have children and live the lives that their parents live.

In spite of the need to get children to think about this, there are deliberately very few examples that push home the point in the selection, and those that do ('Recitative for Punished Products', page 93 and 'The Mechanical Hound', page 103) are quite far removed from their own lives or are treated as a joke. The horrific and the shocking have therefore been avoided. Children have time enough for that. However, I am *not* suggesting that we merely turn our heads the other way — I would hope an alternative, more positive viewpoint is presented in the choice of material. We can admire and delight in Brunel's achievements and gain a sense of the struggle and endurance necessary to achieve anything new. We can all do a job well, with care and pride, and feel satisfied afterwards as Thias does in 'Repairing a Joint' (page 87). And we can all value the thing that we make for ourselves over the thing that is made for us, as in 'Spit Nolan' (page 47).

If this book helps children to look with a new awareness at the things around them; to value themselves and the things they do, as well as the achievements of others, no matter how mundane they seem; to avoid taking for granted what they consider to be the essentials of their lives; and to engage in worthwhile activity in the classroom which they also enjoy, I shall feel I have come near to some of my aims.

All of the material in this book has been tried out in school. Mostly it has been tested in my own school, Sudbury Girls' High School, a girls' comprehensive. The real danger with a theme like this was that it should turn into a boys' book — girls have liked all the pieces. I should like to thank the members of the English Department at the school and many of the children for the ideas, help and encouragement they have given me. The theoretical framework for the book was worked out in close discussion with all the editors of Stage One under the able and helpful chairmanship of Pat Radley. I thank him and Donald Ball, David Jackson, Elwyn Rowlands, George Sanders and Geoffrey Summerfield for their constant boosting and feeding of ideas without which my selection would have been a poor thing. I should also like to thank Martin Lightfoot for his vision and guidance, for the look of the book, and for giving me this opportunity to improve both my thinking and teaching qualitatively. I dedicate *Things Working* to James.

# Books for the Classroom Library

Richard Armstrong, *Sabotage at the Forge* (Dent)

Brian Ball (Editor), *Tales of Science Fiction* (Penguin)

Jean George, *My Side of the Mountain* (Puffin)

*The Penguin Heath Robinson* (Penguin)

Thor Heyerdahl, *Aku-Aku* (Penguin)

Bill Naughton, *The Goalkeeper's Revenge and Other Stories* (Puffin)

E. Nesbit, *The Railway Children* (Puffin)

Clancy Segal, *Weekend in Dinlock* (Penguin)

Geoffrey Summerfield (Editor), *Junior Voices,* 3 and 4 (Penguin)

Jennifer Wayne, *The Day the Ceiling Fell Down* (Puffin)

Laura Ingalls Wilder, *Little House on the Prairie* (Puffin)

# Notes

**Comments by children are in italics**

9  **Wings**

This poem links very closely with the next one because it offers one way of looking at 'who . . . you think you are'.

*What do you feel about yourself after reading this piece?* (This girl went on to talk to a group of friends about the poem and what 'wings' meant to them.)

10  **Machine Head**

*On page 10 I would like to write a poem called 'The World of Confusion'.*

11  **Who do you think you are?**

Look again at the list of what you are made up of, then make a drawing or a collage of what the mixture *might* have looked like if it didn't look like a human. You might use some of the objects mentioned in the poem if you can get hold of them.

Write about things you would *like* to be made of. You might include things like feelings or special qualities like happiness or fun, and you would have to think of a way of measuring them.

12  **I Like That Stuff**

The poem lends itself well to imitation because of its very definite form. A class has made an effective wall display of a class poem, each person contributing one stanza. This had an interesting effect in that the class decided that it gave a full and interesting picture of the nature of their group and felt proud and united because of it. We decided afterwards that wherever possible we should have had some of the actual objects on display (e.g. chocolate, money, books, string) or even stuck on to the poem in place of the central word.

13  **A View of Things**

Bratach Gorm: a blue flag (Gaelic).
etaoin shrdl: compositors type these letters to loosen up, as they are the most commonly used.
setae: bristles.

Although it is similar to 'I Like That Stuff', 'A View of Things' can be handled in a very different way. Again, the pattern of the poem makes imitation appealing, but I have found that it tends to be a much more personal experience; partly because it includes the negative and partly because stronger feelings are involved. The more light-hearted approach of the Mitchell poem makes it easier for it to have a universal application. While one might expect other people to *like* the same things, one's own 'view of things' is very private — though not so private that small groups can't talk very profitably about it.

*Write down your own loves and hates.*

14  **The Easter Islanders Show Thor Heyerdahl How One of Their Giant Statues Was Moved**

toro miro: a plant particular to the Easter Island.
long-ears: white men, prominent citizens on Easter Island who had the lobes of their ears pierced and artificially lengthened so they hung down to their shoulders.

There is much other fascinating material in *Aku-Aku* about the Polynesians and their superstitions and customs. A child who is interested by this passage could go on to read what leads up to it, the creating of one of the giant statues (pages 133–7).

Follow-up work could include writing stories about the original giants, creating a legend about them.

Children could also describe how they would climb one of the statues — What route would you take? Would you cut footholds? Use a rope? Any other equipment? Why might you want to climb the statue?

Further work could be done on primitive man and a fairly lengthy and full project could make use of some of the following suggestions:

Show the first half-hour of the film *2001 – A Space Odyssey* (Metro Goldwyn Meyer, directed by Stanley Kubrick) or take them to see it. The section entitled 'The Dawn of Man' shows early, ape-like man coming across a skeleton. He idly breaks off a bone and with exploding insight realizes that the bone can be used as a club. In slow motion he smashes the skeleton. This superb sequence would show children more clearly than any way I can think of, that things that we take for granted have not always just *been*.

An idea for drama: 'A Million Years Ago the Gift of Fire was Theirs' in *Routes* by W. Martin and G. Vallins (page 1) (Exploration Drama series, published by Evans). Also pages 4–5 on Discovery.

Collect examples of primitive drawings and find out what they tell us about early man.
*Draw very simple designs that could be left on cave walls to tell people in thousands of years' time what we were like.*

*Other Sources*

*The Inheritors* by William Golding (Faber): pages 53–4, 59–60 — on early man finding food.

*The Shield Ring* and *Warrior Scarlet* by Rosemary Sutcliffe (OUP).

18  **Plasticine Sculpture**

Alice only came back to her sculpture a year later when she tried again in plasticine and found it much easier. But disaster befell even that. Her mother entered it for an art competition without her knowing, and it was bought by an unknown purchaser and never seen again! The photograph on pages 20–21 is a clay head in relief and was her fifth attempt.

See also
'How to Paint the Portrait of a Bird' by Jacques Prévert (in *Selected Poems*, Penguin).
'Digging' by Seamus Heaney (in *Death of a Naturalist*, Faber) and 'Mastering the Craft' by Vernon Scannell (*Epithets of War*, Eyre & Spottiswoode) both of these in BBC Pamphlets, *Books, Plays, Poems*, Summer 1970.
*In the Early World* by Elwyn Richardson (New Zealand Education Publications, no. 43) on using clay with children.
'How to Paint a Perfect Christmas' by Miroslav Holub (*Selected Poems*, Penguin). Also in *Voices*, 3, edited by Geoffrey Summerfield (Penguin).

### 24 Carving a Goldfish

Polystyrene is a thick, light, white foamed plastic used in packaging and for insulation.

D. H. Lawrence describes with similar care Mr Morel making pit fuses in *Sons and Lovers* (Penguin), page 83.

See also
'The Goldsmith' by Camara Laye (from *The Dark Child*, translated by James Kirkup in BBC Pamphlets, *Listening and Writing*, Spring 1970).
'The Watch' by May Swenson (in *Half Sun, Half Sleep*, Charles Scribner & Sons and *Junior Voices*, 4, edited by Geoffrey Summerfield, Penguin).

### 25 Jug   sorghum: a kind of molasses.

### 24, 25 Polystyrene and Clay

Look at the backgrounds to these two pages. Try to imagine what it would be like not to be able to see them, but only to feel the surface. Describe the feeling and the texture as your finger runs over the surface.

Look at real examples of polystyrene and clay. Do they in fact look like these pictures of them? What does enlarging do to any surface? Get magnifying glasses and collect as many examples as possible of surfaces in the classroom, e.g. paint, wood, glass, shoe soles, pin-up board, cloth. Make diagrams or write descriptions of how they are made up.

Make a wall display of all the different textures in the room, or on one person in the room.

### 26 The Picket Fence

This rather zany kind of poem lends itself to cartoon comic-strip techniques. There are all sorts of jokes in this vein, like the one about a man who dug a hole in the road and was so proud of it that he put up a FOR SALE notice. A prospective buyer liked it and arranged to have it delivered. A few days later a lorry driver turned up at his house and said there'd been a dreadful accident. 'I dug it up and put it on the back of my lorry,' he said, 'but while I was driving along I hit a bump and it must have fallen off. I didn't realize it at first but when I saw it had gone I went back down the road and fell down it.' This sort of story (of which there are many) could be used as comic-strips and also in dramatic situations.

There is a different translation of this poem in *Junior Voices* 3 (edited by Geoffrey Summerfield, Penguin), page 93. It could be interesting to compare the two.

## 27  The Principle of the Helicopter

The helicopter wasn't the only thing designed in principle by Leonardo. It is amazing to think that in the fifteenth century he was inventing the basis of ball-bearings, the submarine, tanks and various other types of military equipment.

Describe a device available in the fifteenth century which could have been used in a much later invention that is now in common use. Like 'this instrument made with a helix' it could be something that depended on later knowledge to make it work.

## 28, 29, 30  The Bugmobile, A Machine for Travelling over Rough Ground, An Engineer Considers the Problem

These pieces all offer scope for the creative thinking I mentioned in the introduction. Edward de Bono comments on Paul Tant's invention in *Lateral Thinking: A Textbook of Creativity* (Ward Lock), pages 118—20. The essence of children's inventions is that they should not be hidebound by limiting factors but be able to explore the solution of a problem in as open-ended a way as possible. Children delight in inventing as Edward de Bono shows in *The Dog-Exercising Machine* (Penguin), a collection of such inventions. I hope children seeing the ideas in these pages will be encouraged to experiment with their own ideas. With cooperation from art, woodwork and metalwork departments, some of the inventions could be made and tested. Alternatively, scale models could be made in paper. Some girls working with me on the Nuffield *Resources for Learning Project*, on a theme entitled *On the Island*, designed and made inventions to make life easier on the island. There were scale models of a fish-catcher; a trolley made out of sticks and reeds; a shower made out of bamboo poles, a wooden tank and half a coconut punched with holes; paper cups and a water carrier made out of hide. The fun and skill in designing and making these was exciting and very worthwhile.

## 31—5  Heath Robinson

While the other inventions are serious attempts by children to cope with a particular problem, Heath Robinson's inventions delight and enchant children because of their sheer surprise:

*Make up a mad and crazy invention. If it's small try to make it in paper. You could design a machine for keeping your bed warm, eating (if you're lazy!), something to hold your book and turn the pages over, or . . .*

If the first set (pages 28—30) encourage children to think out a practical solution to a problem in a new way, these stimulate children to conceive of something outrageous. After an absence through illness I came back to school one day to find an arrangement on my desk: a bramble, a crisp bag, a belt, a school beret and various other oddments, all falling out of a waste paper basket with a note beneath, 'From Interflora'. It was extraordinarily effective.

Children should have fun with these and suggestions shouldn't be necessary — any children I know run away with themselves when given this opportunity.

Page 34: Write an advertisement for this flat to attract a new tenant (it could be longer than most advertisements).

Page 35: You are commander of the subzeppmarinellin. Make a list of the orders you would give your crew for destroying the enemy.

See also *A Catalogue of Extraordinary Objects* by Jacques Careilman, translated by Rosaleen Walsh (Abelard Schuman).

### 38   Making a Door

Most of Laura Ingalls Wilder's books contain equally clear and informative descriptions of making or doing things, e.g.
Digging a well — *Little House on the Prairie* (pages 105–8) (Puffin).
Making a house — *On the Banks of Plum Creek* (pages 78–80) and milking a cow (pages 32–3) (Puffin).

A passage like this shows that a very close step-by-step description of how to do something need not be boring. It might be useful to look at how the author achieves this effect with any child who tries to do the same thing.

*Other Sources*

Poems
'Starting to Make a Tree' by Roy Fisher (*City,* Migrant Pamphlets, 1961).
How to Paint a Perfect Christmas' and 'The Door' by Miroslav Holub (*Selected Poems,* Penguin).
'The Making of the Horn Spoon' by Gary Snyder (*A Range of Poems,* Fulcrum Press).
'Fine Work with Pitch and Copper' by William Carlos Williams (*Modern Poets 9,* Penguin).
'A Considerable Speck' by Robert Frost (*Complete Poems,* Cape).
'Jazz Fantasia' by Carl Sandburg (*Collected Poems,* Harcourt, Brace & World).
'Negro Spirituals' by James Kirkup (*The Submerged Village,* OUP).
'Thelonius' by Michael Horowitz (*Jazz Poems,* Pocket Poets, Vista Books).
'Personal Helicon' by Seamus Heaney (*Death of a Naturalist,* Faber).
Making a toy model — *Dibs: In Search of Self* (chapter 21) by Virginia Axline (Penguin).
Making wine — *Cider with Rosie* by Laurie Lee, pages 79–80 (Penguin).
Making arrows — *Tom's Midnight Garden* by Philippa Pearce, pages 83–4 (OUP).
Making arrows — *Old Mali and the Boy* by D. R. Sherman, pages 33–40 (Penguin).
Making bread — *Lark Rise to Candleford* by Flora Thompson, pages 35–6 (OUP).
Making Irish Stew — *Three Men in a Boat* by Jerome K. Jerome (Dent).
Making magic — *The Magician's Nephew* by C. S. Lewis (Puffin).
Making figures in a clock — *Armadale* by Wilkie Collins (Cedric Chivers Ltd).
Blacksmith — *Akenfield* by Ronald Blythe (Allen Lane The Penguin Press).
*My Side of the Mountain* by Jean George (Puffin).
*Something to Do* by Septima (Puffin).

### 39   The Garden Door

The response by children to this door has been mixed. While some have seen it simply as an illustration of the door that Laura's Pa made, others have seen it as a threat, as if they are being shut out. Many have therefore wanted to write about what or who is behind it and have made up stories about the people involved:

*Who lives behind this door? Write about the family's adventures.*
*Which side would you rather be on?*

**41—65** The next section is about one of the more common aspects of 'things' —
the machines about us. A local secondary school has harnessed the
fascination that most children feel for machines very effectively, by
using 'Industry' as a theme for an integrated project with the whole of
the first year.

In four groups the children went to different factories having previously
been briefed about what to look for. On their return to school they spent
the best part of two days working either individually or in small groups at
sessions of music, art, written English and drama, joining or leaving each
group under the direction of a teacher. Eventually, after all the children
had spent some time on each activity, they met together in the hall to
display the results — pieces of writing were read out, pinned up, acted or
taped: paintings were displayed, so were some fairly complex machines
which had been designed out of oddments of materials: some made music,
others had taped their efforts, one pair even combined this with the
movement of the machine itself and the whole project ended up with a
lively improvised dramatization of the Peterloo Massacre.

Although there are obvious drawbacks in timetabling and administration,
this sort of integrated work does engender its own enthusiasm and can
carry the children on the crest of a wave to produce better and better
work — this is one way of dealing with this section *en masse*.

**42 TV Man**

*Make a face from a TV screen or other similar object. Have a competition*
*if enough do it with prizes. Write a poem about your picture describing it.*

**44 Knob**

verger: in the sense of one who acts as an attendant who takes care of the
interior.

Children often enjoy making up short concrete poems about everyday
objects. We have made an alphabet of poems of things we couldn't do
without, e.g. aerosol, light bulb, zip. One could also use things to make
life easier or things we *could* do without.

Children enjoy playing with words and ideas and can be stimulated by the
simplest things, like these words from a Midland Bank advertisement:

# br⁻dge train
# aut₀m₀bile

and come up with ideas like:

# biOyCle Pram

An example follows from our alphabet:

*LIGHT OF NIGHT* ... *BRIGHT PIERCING* ... *to GLARE.* ... *TRANSPARENT* ... *CLEAR GLASS* ... *SUN IN A GLASS* ... *FALSE SUNLIGHT* ... *LIGHT* ... *LIFE LINE* ... *DARK ... TO DAY ...*

*Jane Clarke, 14 years, Sudbury Girls' High School*

See also *The Word as Image* by Berjouhi Bowler (Studio Vista).

*Concrete Poems*

*The Second Life* by Edwin Morgan (Edinburgh University Press).
*Vaughan Papers No. 13: Concrete Poetry* edited by Ronald Draper
(University of Leicester, 22½p — write direct for copies).

**45 Glasses**

This poem opens up possibilities for talking and writing about other evil
necessities, e.g. teeth braces. The intensity of feeling involved is aptly
shown in the following defensive suggestion by a girl who wears glasses:
*Draw the other side of the pair of glasses and write lines in favour of
glasses.*

I have approached the poem in two ways: through acting, we have looked
at the different reactions children have when they are told they will have
to wear glasses, plaster for a broken leg or teeth braces.

A small group of children (four) were given the poem and asked to record
their discussion of it on tape. They were alone, as I left them to it, and the
talk that developed was both intimate and supportive as they went on to
talk about the things that make them feel self-conscious.

## 47 Spit Nolan

This story captures, in a way which few of today's children really know, the sense of making something yourself and making it yours — you simply don't have things made *for* you.

I have found that children are moved and impressed by this story and find much to talk about. After reading it to a whole class once I found they were very subdued by it, but after improvising alternative endings, could detach themselves sufficiently to talk about it enthusiastically and openly. I find it is this use of drama which often brings children to terms with something they find upsetting so they can eventually say, 'Oh well, it is only a story'.

## 56 The Old Allon

I have deliberately left the extract open-ended but for any children who would like to know what happened, Wiggin had great difficulty stopping the Allon. He ploughed through a herd of cows, going (he says) underneath one. The engine conveniently cut out, but just as he was about to stop, cut in again and eventually he and the Allon splashed into a brook. (*In Spite of the Price of Hay*, OUP, pages 152–4).

While this extract might be of specialist interest mainly to boys, it also stands as an adventure in its own right. I have had one girl explain so enthusiastically what all the components are in the picture on page 57 that she even turned over the page to show me what was on the other side of the engine!

## 60 The Last Great Tram Race

This has been abridged from an article which appeared in the *Weekend Telegraph* on 1 April, 1966. The following week it was announced that it was an April Fool hoax and that there have never been tram races in Liverpool.

See also
'The Yo-Yo Championship' by Frank Conroy (from *Stop-Time,* published by Viking Press Inc. and in B B C pamphlet *Listening and Writing,* Spring 1970).
'The First, Last and Only Hyde Park Grand Prix' — in *Car* Magazine, June 1968.

## 64 The Makers of Speed

litany: public prayer

This poem can be used effectively as choral verse with movement, with groups of children representing the workmen and others stylized machines. Music could carry it on into a much larger dramatic experience.

*Other sources for material in this general section*

Poems
'A Chinese Toy' by William Carlos Williams (*Collected Earlier Poems,* MacGibbon & Kee).
'Bicycles' by Andrei Voznesensky (*Antiworlds,* OUP).
'Churning Day' by Seamus Heaney (*Death of a Naturalist,* Faber).

'End of a Harvest Day' by John Hurst (*Every Man will Shout* edited by R. Mansfield and I. Armstrong, OUP).
'I Know a Man' by Robert Creeley (*Contemporary American Poetry,* Penguin).
'Out West' by Gary Snyder (*A Range of Poems,* Fulcrum Press).
'The Secret of the Machines' and 'The Deep Sea Cables' by Rudyard Kipling (*Complete Poems,* Hodder & Stoughton).
'Out, Out . . .' by Robert Frost (*Complete Poems,* Cape).
'The Green Train' by E. V. Rieu (*Puffin Quartet of Poets*).
'The Water-Wheel' by Jack Clemo (*Penguin Modern Poets 6*).
*The Poetry of Railways* edited by K. Hopkins (Leslie Frewin).

Making irrigation hand pumps out of bicycles – *The Ugly American* by W. Lederer and E. Burdick, chapter 18 (Corgi).
Looking through a microscope – *The Thurber Carnival* by James Thurber (Penguin).
Furnace room, cinder track – *A London Childhood* by John Holloway (Routledge & Kegan Paul).
The furnace, the boiler room, the control room – *The Excitement of Writing* by A. B. Clegg (Chatto & Windus).
Gas engines – *In Spite of the Price of Hay* by Maurice Wiggin (OUP).
Using a telephone – *The Watchers and the Watched* by Sid Chaplin, page 207 (Panther).
Threshing machine – *Thimble Summer* by Elizabeth Enright (Puffin).
Being run over by a train – *Dombey and Son* by Charles Dickens (Penguin).
Seeing a train for the first time – *The Good Master* by Kate Seredy (Harrap).
Seeing a train as a dragon – 'The Dragon' in *The Day it Rained Forever* by Ray Bradbury (Penguin).
*The Railway Children* by E. Nesbit (Puffin).
*The Railway Game* by Clifford Dyment (Dent). (BBC pamphlet, *Listening and Writing,* Summer 1969).
Paper-machine – 'The Tartarus of Maids' in *Complete Stories of Herman Melville,* pages 205–7 (Eyre & Spottiswoode).
*A Clockwork Orange* by Anthony Burgess (Heinemann).
Motor-bikes – *In Spite of the Price of Hay* by Maurice Wiggin (OUP).
Motor-bikes – *Collected Letters of T. E. Lawrence* (Cape).
Steam engines – *The Ballad of John Axon* (Argo Records, RG474).
Steam trawlers – *Life on the Mississippi* by Mark Twain, chapter 20 (Chatto & Windus).
*Wings: An Anthology of Flight* edited by H. Bryden (Faber).

**66    Construction for Isambard Kingdom Brunel**

Amongst other things, Isambard Kingdom Brunel designed and built twenty-five railways in England, Ireland, Italy and India, eight piers and dry docks, five suspension bridges and 125 railway bridges.

Concrete poetry gives free rein to children's natural inventiveness, but still requires a very conscious and often precise use of language. I don't often advocate close textual examination, but a look at the way Morgan uses language in this poem could encourage some exciting work.

*Write your christian name and surname, leave the christian name alone and deal with the surname to find out how your name originated, then copy on to a piece of paper.*

Although this girl took little of the meaning of the poem, her idea is a possible way of getting children to play with words, in this case their own names.

### 71 O Pioneers!

An early attempt to start a Channel Tunnel at Dover in 1880 was abandoned. Since then there have been many plans and decisions but the Channel Tunnel has still not been started.

Strangely enough, the photograph has made most children think of gravestones, and may need its significance pointed out.

### 72 Coal-Mine

*The Road to Wigan Pier* offers much other suitable material on coal mines as does Clancy Segal's *Weekend in Dinlock* (Penguin).

### 74 Mining Rhyming

Mining isn't the only sphere in which song-making was popular although it has its own very rich tradition. In some mines, if you were addressed in rhyme you were expected to answer in rhyme.

Collect examples of work songs by asking fathers and grandfathers or going further afield. Many Negro spirituals are in fact work songs and there are also many African and Caribbean examples. If it is possible to get hold of the tunes, make a taped collection of the songs rather than a written one.

The picture on this page could lead to interesting discussions about the conditions in which people work.

A small group of children could conduct a small survey with the help of a portable tape-recorder by interviewing people about their work conditions. In school, this could include the secretary, the caretaker, a sixth former, the window cleaner, the Head, the P.E. teacher, a cleaner. Or the children could go further afield to find a wider range of jobs.

### 75 Pit Pony

*Write a song to accompany any job you often do, e.g. delivering newspapers, washing-up, cleaning the car, sorting stamps.*

See also: Pete Seeger: *Songs of Work and Freedom* (now out of production) (Transatlantic records).

Find examples of rhyming slang particular to certain occupations, e.g. Yorkshire tyke: mike (i.e. microphone, used by radio and TV technicians). Windjammer: hammer (used by carpenters working on film sets). Paddy Rammer: hammer (cockney workmen). Lord Lovell: shovel.

Find out what people have to do in jobs you don't know about. What does a die stamper do? A fitter? A radiographer?

### 76 The Ballad of the Big Hewer

This radio ballad is put out by Argo records (RG538) who have also produced other song documentaries: *The Ballad of John Axon* (RG474),

*Fight Game* (RG539), *Singing the Fishing* (RG502). The form of the song documentary, a combination of a main song interspersed with shorter complete songs, anecdotes, jokes and comments on one main theme is one that lends itself admirably to classroom use. With the cooperation of a music teacher, the tune of any well-known and easily available folk song can be used as the basis for the children's own song documentary. Some sort of local emphasis would be helpful as children could go out with a portable tape-recorder and ask people in the area for their comments — possibilities would be the steam engine (as in *John Axon*), the penny farthing, old farm machinery (as described in George Ewart Evans's books *The Horse in the Furrow*, *Ask the Fellows Who cut the Hay*, *The Farm and the Village* (Faber)), horses, barges, trawlers or any other local speciality. A project of this nature need not only be for listening to (as in a radio ballad) — it could be a dramatized version like *Close the Coalhouse Door* by Alan Plater (Methuen).

I have used this idea on a small scale with a group of fifth formers who did a post-examination project on a disused local railway line. It can be fun, is chaotic to organize and does depend on the children working well in groups and being committed. These girls were a bit apathetic and didn't do too well.

## 78—81  The Ballad of the Big Hewer

These comments are all from miners. Children attempting to produce their own documentary might use this idea of eliciting comments from people, or by interviewing them.

## 82  News

The extract is from *Close the Coalhouse Door* by Alan Plater (Methuen). It offers wide scope for dramatic improvisation, either as a continuation or simply as a comment on the tenseness of language spoken in stress.

*Other Sources*

Poems
*The Collier* by Vernon Watkins (Faber).
'Caliban in the Coal Mines' by Louis Untermeyer (*The Long Feud*, Harcourt Brace & World).
'The Excavation' by Max Endicoff (*The New Republic*).
'The Spring' by Gary Snyder (*A Range of Poems*, Fulcrum Press).
'Factory Windows are Always Broken' by Vachel Lindsay (*Collected Poems*, Macmillan).
'Classic Scene' by William Carlos Williams (*Collected Earlier Poems*, MacGibbon & Kee).
'North Kent' by Thom Gunn (*Listener*, 22 February 1968).
*Thaw on a Building Site* by Norman MacCaig.
'Wild Iron' by Allen Curnow (*A Book of New Zealand Verse 1923—45*, The Caxton Press).
*Collected Poems of Carl Sandburg* (Harcourt, Brace & World).

Records
TOP74: *The Collier's Rant: Mining Songs of Northumbrian and Durham Coalfields* by Louis Killen and Johnny Handle (Topic).
12T86: *The Iron Muse* — industrial songs (Topic).

12T134: *Move On Down the Line* — work-songs (Topic).
12T189: *Along the Coaly Tyne* — Louis Killen and Johnny Handle (Topic).

Coal-mining
*The Bonnie Pit Laddie* by Frederick Grice (OUP).
*The Road to Wigan Pier* by George Orwell (Penguin).
*The Whinstone Drift* by Richard Armstrong (Dent).
*One Small Boy* by Bill Naughton (Panther).
*Weekend in Dinlock* by Clancy Segal (Penguin).
'Farewell to the Monty' by Johnny Handle (*Modern Folk Ballads*, Pocket
Poets, Vista; sung on *The Iron Muse*, Topic Records).

Railway
*The Railway Navvies* by Terry Coleman (Penguin).
*Red for Danger* by L. T. C. Rolt (Longman).

Oil
*Campbell's Kingdom* by Hammond Innes (Collins).

Waterways
*Inland Waterways* by L. T. C. Rolt (Educational Supply Association).
*Kariba* by Frank Clements (Methuen).
*The Lives of Bolton and Watt* by Samuel Smiles (Murray).
*Isambard Kingdom Brunel* by L. T. C. Rolt (Penguin).
*Engineering Magic* by Garry Hogg (Abelard Schuman).
*Hard Times* by Charles Dickens (Penguin).

**84  Pig at Machine**

This extract is from *Smallcreep's Day* by Peter C. Brown (Panther), a very
bizarre and almost Kafka-esque novel which would not be suitable for
children in this age group except in odd extracts like this one and a
description of 'pipes' (pages 13—14). All the same, the *idea* of the novel
could be used in school. Pinkuah Smallcreep, a manual worker in a factory,
decides to see what is happening in the rest of the factory on one day. A
group of children could equally decide to see what is really happening in
their school on any one particular day — what does the Head's secretary
do? The school nurse, the caretaker, the cook, the gardener, the teachers
in a free period? What other people visit the school? Parents, delivery men,
doctor, publishers' reps; what happens in the staff room or the boiler
room and so on. An enlightening and probably amusing report could
come out of such observations, especially if a tape-recording was made
of interviews with some of the people. Ideally film could be used as well,
or closed-circuit television.

**90  Bench Dreams**

From 'On the Line' by Bryan Slater which is one of several people's
accounts of their jobs in *Work* edited by Ronald Fraser (Penguin).

Children are, not surprisingly, in sympathy with this piece because they
so often feel bored. We have talked a good deal about day-dreaming as
a result of reading this.

**91  Machine Operators**

Assuming that children these days know something about Charlie Chaplin,
this picture should stimulate some fairly inventive and hair-raising
dramatic possibilities.

## 92 Aeroplane Dump

This is a photograph of a mound of obsolete U S A F aircraft. Children are incredulous and horrified that it isn't in fact a joke and have talked about pollution (it appeared as an illustration to an article on pollution in *Horizon,* an American journal) and waste disposal.

## 93 Recitative for Punished Products

This has been very successfully used as choral verse, spoken and enacted formally and in a very stylized way. It could be further developed into a dance drama with music. Otherwise it highlights an aspect of 'things working' which was consciously avoided elsewhere in the book.

## 94 Found Poem

It is interesting to note that this 'found poem' by Jean L'Anselme was originally 'found' — unknown to L'Anselme — a few years before by Gerard Hoffnung, the great cartoonist and humorist, who gave it wide currency and popularity in Britain.

## 98 Doing Nothing

This is from *Where did you go? Out. What did you do? Nothing* by Robert Paul Smith (The World's Work). It is an American book, not easily available in this country, but it does contain a wealth of marvellous childhood reminiscences and descriptions of what the author used to do. See particularly pages 41–3, 107–11, 32–9, 117–27.

A question like 'what do you do when you do nothing?' has provoked endless talk, including tricky philosophical ventures into what we mean by 'nothing'!

## 99 Boy in Street   *Is this boy 'doing nothing'? What could he be doing?*

## 84–99

These pages were all concerned with people at work, of one kind and another. It would be a pity in a book like this, not to include the people who make other kind of discoveries — the explorers. Much of this material is readily accessible and difficult to extract successfully and therefore I include it here as a list, with a few other examples.

*Other Sources*

'Somebody has to Make Tubs and Pails' from *The People, Yes* by Carl Sandburg (Harcourt, Brace & World).
'New Farm Tractor' by Carl Sandburg (*Collected Poems of Carl Sandburg,* Harcourt, Brace & World).
'The House Builder at Work' from *Song of the Broad Axe* by Walt Whitman.
'A Song for Occupations' by Walt Whitman (*Leaves of Grass,* Dent).
'Oil', '7: VII' and 'Fire in the Hole' by Gary Snyder (*A Range of Poems,* Fulcrum Press).
'The Swan-Necked Valve' on *The Iron Muse* (Topic Records).
'Bathymeter' by W. Hart-Smith (*Penguin Book of Australian Verse*).
'Alex at the Barber's' by John Fuller (*Fairground Music,* Chatto & Windus).
'Transplanting' and 'Old Florist' by Theodore Roethke (*Complete Poems,* Faber).

'Digging', 'The Diviner' and 'Scaffolding' by Seamus Heaney (*Death of a Naturalist*, Faber).
'Death on a Live Wire' by Michael Baldwin (*Sense and Sensitivity* by Patrick Creber, Longman).
'The Wheel King' by Howard Nemerov (*Mirrors and Windows*, University of Chicago Press).
'In Back of the Real' by Allen Ginsberg (*Howl and Other Poems*, City Lights Books, San Francisco).
'A Truthful Song' by Rudyard Kipling (*Complete Poems*, Hodder & Stoughton).
'The Release' by W. W. Gibson (*The Golden Room and Other Poems*, Macmillan).

The sea
*The Secret Sea*, *Sea Change* and *Danger Rock* by Richard Armstrong (Dent).
*Half Mile Down* by William Beebe (Bodley Head).
*The Bombard Story* by Alain Bombard (André Deutsch).
*The Silent World* by J. J. Cousteau (Hamish Hamilton).
*Alone Across the Atlantic* by Francis Chichester (Allen & Unwin).
*The Lonely Sea and the Sky* by Francis Chichester (Hodder & Stoughton).
*Moby Dick* by Herman Melville (Collins), whale-hunting.
*South Latitude* by F. S. Ommaney (Longman), whale-hunting.
*The Kon-Tiki Expedition* by Thor Heyerdahl (Allen & Unwin).
*The Bird of Dawning* by John Masefield (Heinemann).
*Maiden's Trip* by Emma Smith (Peacock).
*Swallows and Amazons* by Arthur Ransome (Puffin).
*20,000 Leagues Under the Sea* by Jules Verne (Dent).
*The Mary Deare* by Hammond Innes (Collins).

The air
*Sagittarius Rising* by Cecil Lewis (Peter Davies).
*Reach for the Sky* by Paul Brickhill (Collins).
*Vol de Nuit* by Antoine de Saint-Exupéry (*Night-Flying* translated by Stuart Gilbert, Crosby Continental Edition).

Mountains
*Annapurna* by Maurice Herzog (Cape).
*The Ascent of Everest* by Sir John Hunt.
*The Crossing of Antarctica* by Sir Vivian Fuchs (Cassell).

Farm and rural life
*Ask the Fellows Who cut the Hay*, *The Horse in the Furrow* and *The Farm and the Village* by George Ewart Evans (Faber).
*Akenfield* by Ronald Blythe (Allen Lane The Penguin Press).

Machines
*The Watchers on the Shore* by Stan Barstow, pages 76–80 (Penguin).
*The Beginners* by Dan Jacobson (Penguin), butter factory.
*The Torrents of Spring* by Ernest Hemingway (Penguin), pump factory.

People
*Seven Years Solitary* by Edith Bone (Hamish Hamilton).
*The Radium Woman* by Eleanor Doorley (Heinemann).
*Men who Shaped the Future* by Egon Larsen (Dent).
*Men who Changed the World* by Egon Larsen (Dent).
*The Diary of a Nobody* by George and Weedon Grossmith (Penguin).

### 100 Used Trout Stream

While on one level this passage may be too sophisticated for some of the children in this age range, they do respond very well to the utter craziness of it. Children who have read this like the way the suspension of disbelief is kept up in such a flat, unadorned way and I have had some very interesting writing as a result — unfortunately too long to be able to reprint here.

### 103 The Mechanical Hound

I have seen a comic-strip version of this story that works very well.

Some children like to write or act the next instalment and once *that* was made into a comic-strip too.

### 105 Japanese War God

*Write an imaginary story of a 'thing' which came down and ruled the earth. What devices did it use? Imagine you got rid of it without killing. How?*

Because some children find the Paolozzi sculpture disturbing or threatening, they need to explain it away. Story-writing helps here, so does improvised drama, because they can always win.

### 106 Life in the Machine

Design a machine which you think you could live in happily, making sure you have provided for all your needs.

If you were to 'get . . . ideas in an airship' what might they be?

### 108 The Computer's Second Christmas Card

*Write your own message in the way Edwin Morgan's computer wrote his.*

*Write something that* looks *a load of nonsense, is* a load of nonsense, sounds *a load of nonsense, but makes sense.*

See also
'The Computer's First Christmas Card' in *The Second Life* by Edwin Morgan (Edinburgh University Press). This has been widely anthologized. A ten-year-old produced her own version, of which I reproduce a short part:

**The Computer's Halloween**

| | |
|---|---|
| Witches broom stick | sitches room |
| stick witch broom | stickers doom |
| broom stick witch | stick black |
| broom stack witch | black stick |
| stick broom stack | plot stick |
| stick broom wack | broom stick |
| wacker stick | broom wick |
| pitcherstick | snick pick |
| spickerboom | broomfick |
| picker boom | broomfire |
| pitches broom | fire broom |
| witches broom | firebroomfick |
| witches room | fickbroomfire |
| | witches fire |

It goes on for three foolscap columns.

```
MERRY CHRISTMAS EVERYONE          ** HIGHDOWN LC
MERRY CHRISTMAS EVERYONE
MERRY CHRISTMAS EVERYONE
MERRY CHRISTMAS EVERYONE
MERRY CHRISTMAS EVERYONE
MERRY CHRISTMAS EVERYONE          *S FATHER CHRISTMAS
MERRY CHRISTMAS EVERYONE
MERRY CHRISTMAS EVERYONE
MERRY CHRISTMAS EVERYONE
MERRY CHRISTMAS EVERYONE
MERRY CHRISTMAS EVERYONE          [MESSAGE]
MERRY CHRISTMAS EVERYONE          WORDS  EMER
MERRY CHRISTMAS EVERYONE              ERY
MERRY CHRISTMAS EVERYONE              ECHR
MERRY CHRISTMAS EVERYONE              EIST
MERRY CHRISTMAS EVERYONE              EMAS
MERRY CHRISTMAS EVERYONE              E EV
MERRY CHRISTMAS EVERYONE              EERY
MERRY CHRISTMAS EVERYONE              EONE
MERRY CHRISTMAS EVERYONE          OK  +0
MERRY CHRISTMAS EVERYONE          MESSAGE 4 -100
MERRY CHRISTMAS EVERYONE           5 OK
MERRY CHRISTMAS EVERYONE          SNOW 4 +24
MERRY CHRISTMAS EVERYONE           11 QCHAR
MERRY CHRISTMAS EVERYONE            8 QCHAR+1
MERRY CHRISTMAS EVERYONE           /0 WORDS
MERRY CHRISTMAS EVERYONE           10 OK
MERRY CHRISTMAS EVERYONE            6 OK
MERRY CHRISTMAS EVERYONE            9 SNOW
MERRY CHRISTMAS EVERYONE          BELLS 8 BELLS
MERRY CHRISTMAS EVERYONE          X
MERRY CHRISTMAS EVERYONE
MERRY CHRISTMAS EVERYONE
MERRY CHRISTMAS EVERYONE
MERRY CHRISTMAS EVERYONE
MERRY CHRISTMAS EVERYONE
MERRY CHRISTMAS EVERYONE
MERRY CHRISTMAS EVERYONE
MERRY CHRISTMAS EVERYONE
MERRY CHRISTMAS EVERYONE
MERRY CHRISTMAS EVERYONE
MERRY CHRISTMAS EVERYONE
MERRY CHRISTMAS EVERYONE
ME

        *** TIME LIMIT EXCEEDED ***
```

At a much more sophisticated level is the poem on the previous page produced by a pupil of David Miller's at Highdown School, Reading. It was produced as part of a Lower Sixth Computer Science Course after seeing Edwin Morgan's poem.

The message itself consists of 'Merry Christmas Everyone' printed a hundred times (in theory).

In order to get the computer to do this, the following flow diagram must be used:

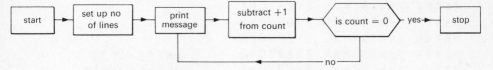

The sheet beginning 'Father Christmas' is the computer's instructions (coding sheet).

1. The word in brackets tells the computer to start.
2. The £ sign indicates the letters of the message.
3. The Second 'Message' sets up the count (100 in this case).
4. 'Snow' to 'Words' tells it to print the words all on one line.
5. Down to the next 'Snow' tells the computer to print and count.
6. 'Bells' repeated on the same line tells the computer to stop.

The Christmas words used in the coding sheet are known as 'identifiers' and tell the computer where in the instructions to go next.

Not only is it 'successful'; the identifiers are a sort of mechanical pun.

**110    Spacepoem I: from Laika to Gagarin**

Laika, a dog, was the first living creature to go up in a space ship.
Yuri Gagarin was the first human being to go up in a space ship.

*What do you think this means: is it a code, is it a language, is it space radio interference, is it, is it?*

Does it matter?

**112–17    Moonwords**

This is a verbatim transcript of some of the first words spoken on the moon. We end where we began. Man landed on the moon on 21 July 1969. The magnitude of this achievement has quickly become accepted and soon will be taken for granted.

One way to keep these sorts of achievements fresh for children is to get them to re-examine some of the things in their own lives and imagine a conversation that might have taken place at the time of the first telephone call, the first television programme, the first ride in an aeroplane.

Make up a glossary of technical or jargon words used at school, in a doctor's surgery, in a shop and write a conversation using them, or make a chart explaining them.

Record this conversation on tape as if it were all happening now.

**118    Off Course**

Very successful comic strips can be made of the story behind this poem.

I read it with a group of thirteen to fourteen-year-old girls who were so upset about the men being condemned to die in limbo that they created a planet for them to land on. This project took a term – they built a model of the planet, designed houses, people, animals and plants and, in groups, worked out the geographical, sociological, biological, psychological, anthropological basis for the society – ending up with a book combining all the material and the models on display to the school. It was an immensely exciting experience and forced them to touch on really basic philosophical concepts, e.g. at first they decided to make their race superior to the human race but then decided that perfect beings would be too boring!

A small group also spent a great deal of time talking about the poem and recording their views – they found it a rewarding and exploratory experience and increased the depth of their approach to the poem. They were on their own to do this and it would probably have been less successful in a large group.

### Extracts from the book on Tenalp – a new planet

*How Tenalp was Formed*
When the earth was young and just cooling down the gases that were being forced out caused a tremendous explosion. Many pieces broke off the earth and drifted away. One of these pieces was extra large and it drifted away towards the sun. All the living things on this breakaway planet that survived the explosion were unicellular. When the planet drifted near to the sun the side of the planet nearest the sun received special cifitneics rays which made the unicellular creatures on that side of the planet join together to form an immobile mass with amazing intelligence. This was how the governing influence of Tenalp was formed.

*Houses in Tenalp*
The houses in Tenalp are icosahedron shaped. They are made of a strong polaroid-type glass so the occupiers can see out but passers-by cannot see in. They are joined to a stalk made of strong opaque material. These, in turn, are joined to tubes which are used as roads. The houses easily sink into the ground at curfew time. They sink into the ground through their stalks.

*Off Course*
After the initial shock
Of the awful jarring thud
Time seemed to stand still.
I looked at my companions
And saw my sick horror
Reflected in their eyes.
We did not speak, or try to think.
We just floated in utter silence
And were.
Then we spoke together,
Stopped and apologized foolishly
For being.

*Other Sources*

Reality
*Children of the Ashes* by Robert Jungk (Penguin).
*Brighter than 1,000 Suns* by Robert Jungk (Penguin).
*Americans in Space* by John Dille (American Heritage Publishing Company).
*Wonders of Gravity* by Rocco Fuarolo (A. Wheats & Co., Exeter).
*The Story of Computers* by Roger Piper (Brockhampton).
*All about Space Flight* by Harold L. Goodwin (W. H. Allen).
*Space Travel* by G. V. Groves.

N A S A – the National Aeronautics and Space Administration in Washington will send an enormous amount of material on space flight on request: posters, pamphlets, booklets, bibliographies, etc.

Fiction

*A Wrinkle in Time* by Madeleine L'Engle (Puffin).
*Dandelion Wine* by Ray Bradbury (Corgi).
*Golden Apples of the Sun* by Ray Bradbury (Corgi).
*The Silver Locusts* by Ray Bradbury (Corgi).
*The Day It Rained Forever* by Ray Bradbury (Penguin).
*Tiger! Tiger!* by Alfred Bester (Penguin).
*The Wind from Nowhere* by J. G. Ballard (Penguin).
*Who?* by Algis Budrys (Penguin).
*Sands of Mars, The Other Side of the Sky* and *Earthlight* by Arthur C. Clarke (Pan).
*Mandrake* by Susan Cooper (Penguin).
*Man of Double Deed* by Leonard Daventry (Penguin).
*Billion Dollar Brain* by Len Deighton (Penguin).
*First Men on the Moon* and *The Time Machine* by H. G. Wells (Collins).
*The Outward Urge* by John Wyndham and Lucas Parkes (Penguin).
*Tales of Science Fiction* edited by Brian Ball (Penguin).
*Moon Creatures* by Ted Hughes (B B C pamphlets *Listening and Writing*, Autumn 1966).

# Ventures
## Elwyn Rowlands

A 'sense of adventure' is part of the make-up of every human being. In adults it varies greatly from individual to individual — from, for example, at one extreme, a passive sense of wonderment at the achievement of landing on the moon, to, at the other extreme, what seems to amount to an absolute necessity to sail single-handed round the world. In children such a variation is not nearly as marked: on the contrary, a strong and active sense of adventure seems critical to their development. At the age of eleven and twelve such a sense assumes a particular significance because they are on the bridge between childhood and adolescence. They are concerned and interested to explore, talk about, act out, write about, not only their own adventures, but also the adventures of others — and this in some more realistic way than they did at earlier ages. The child who at the age of six or seven really imagined that one day he would build a space-ship and go to the moon, and who collected pieces of equipment for such an exploit, has, by the age of eleven, reached the stage where he sees things more realistically and yet still very much in his own terms. Any imaginative exploration he now makes of a journey to the moon is still subjective: he will make it in terms of what *he* knows of the world and the way it works. He has not yet reached the stage of being sufficiently objective to realize that many aspects of such a journey are beyond his comprehension.

Interestingly, in Power', Jack Cope makes André, who is ten, fill '. . . the empty spaces in his life by imagining things'.

He saw an Everest film once and for a long time he was Hillary or Tensing, or both, conquering the mountain. There were no mountains so he conquered the roof of the house which wasn't very high and was made of red-painted tin. But he reached the summit and planted a flag on the lightning conductor. When he got down his mother hit his legs with a quince switch for being naughty.

Another time he conquered the koppie. It took him the whole afternoon to get there and back and it was not as exciting as he expected, being less steep than it looked from a distance, so he did not need his rope and pick. Also, he found a cow had beaten him to the summit.

Cope's psychological insight seems to me to be right: ' . . . his mother hit his legs with a quince switch for being naughty' and ' . . . so he did not need his rope and pick. Also, he found a cow had beaten him to the summit' are accurately suggestive of a sense of reality that is beginning to overtake a child at this age. Most children of eleven and twelve are sufficiently older than André to see the humour in 'so he did not need his rope and pick' and 'a cow had beaten him to the summit'. The word 'naughty' is one they very decidedly associate with their past; and yet they are still near enough to André's age and consequent sensibilities to remember them in themselves.

One of the mistakes I think we are often inclined to make when dealing with pupils at this age, which is probably a result of our not knowing which camp – of childhood or adolescence – they belong to, is that of imagining that they respond in some essentially different way to what they regard as adventures in their own lives and to what we, as adults, regard as adventures. For us a child's fears on being stuck in a tree and somebody's emotional response to scaling the North Face of the Eiger, for example, are so different as to have virtually nothing in common. For the eleven year old this is not so. They can move remarkably easily from a consideration of Scott returning from the South Pole to a discussion about adventures they have had in exceptionally snowy weather. The fact ought not to be surprising: their only means of measuring what they don't know is on terms of what they do. Any real adventure is still likely to be seen to some extent as a story rather than an established fact, a piece of history. Only gradually does their own fiction about the world turn to some sense of truth; and it is now that questions like 'what is it really like?' are starting to be asked much more frequently. Scott, while still being the hero in an adventure story, is gradually becoming a real man, who made a real journey in a place that really does exist. However, I believe it is only through a projection of their own sense of what it is like to be cold, what it is to be tired, what friendship means to them, and so on, that the one replaces the other. Our job is to gradually prompt and feed the sense of reality while being careful to preserve and enhance the sense of wonder. I hope this will answer any objection that, say, 'Return to Air' and Alan Moorehead are strange mixers. For us they may be; for children of eleven and twelve I don't believe they are. On the contrary, they seem to be necessary the one to the other if there is to be any overall exploration of what adventure means at this age. The boy of eleven who swims fifteen lengths at the local baths one weekend, to the point of what he believes to be exhaustion, is not unlikely to have day-dreams about swimming the Channel one day; the boy who scores three goals for the Junior Eleven in a vital cup match and becomes a hero for the day is not unlikely to imagine himself one day stepping onto the turf at Wembley. Such day-dreaming, projection into the future, is important as an exploration of possibilities. Our task is to introduce the more realistic element of probability but we need to do it with a maximum of tact and good sense. There is something wrong with a boy of fourteen or fifteen who still eats, drinks and sleeps football to the exclusion of all else, particularly if he is an only average player: his sense of reality is underdeveloped. The boy of eleven can be, needs to be, indulged to some extent: what he is doing is playing with possibilities and this is important for his growth. He is at the delicate stage mid-way between that of the six year old who asks you to join him (next year!) on his expedition to Lapland to see the reindeer and the sixth former who can begin realistically to plan such an expedition. An almost totally unrealistic notion about possibilities is developing into a proper curiosity about probabilities. Reality and unreality still go very much hand in hand however, and it is right that they should be allowed to do so.

The book contains selections with which pupils will very readily identify: 'Return to Air', 'The Barn', 'The Tree' – selections to which they will be able to say 'I've had experience like that', 'I've been in that sort of situation'. I hope they will lead to plenty of talk, drama and further writing: that they will be starting points. The book moves to selections which are progressively further removed from the pupils' experiences: 'The Bicycle Race', 'A Mining Man', 'The Bear', Alan Moorehead, all of which, I hope, while feeding the sense of adventure and providing plenty of opportunities for activities in the English lesson, also answer the question 'what is it really like?' ('I know what it's like to ride my bike 'til I'm very tired, what's it like to ride to the point of exhaustion?'; 'I know what it's like to face a frightening dog, what's it like to face a bear?' and so on). It is important that contrasts are made, connections established, similarities pointed out: only by playing about with ideas and notions, are children likely to begin to understand.

If it is not too obvious a point to make, I hope the book will be used in an adventurous way: that the teacher will allow ideas to breed, that he will take his main cues about the way to proceed from the children themselves, that he will let them teach him what it is they are concerned to explore. The need is for an experimental, open-ended, opportunist approach, a reading of the signs as they come along.

# Books for the Classroom Library

James Vance Marshall, *Walkabout* (Peacock)

Marjorie Kinnon Rawlings, *The Yearling* (Peacock)

Eric Williams, *Great Escape Stories* (Peacock)

Bill Naughton, *The Goalkeeper's Revenge and Other Stories* (Puffin)

Bernard Newman (ed.), *People Living Dangerously* (Paul Hamlyn)

*The Guinness Book of Records*

An Atlas

Paul Edwards (ed.), *Best Sports Stories* (Faber)

Michael Baldwin, *Grandad with Snails* (Hutchinson)

Ian Seraillier, *The Silver Sword* (Puffin)

Meindert DeJong, *The House of Sixty Fathers* (Puffin)

Anne Holm, *I Am David* (Peacock)

D. R. Sherman, *Old Mali and The Boy* (Penguin)

# Notes

### 6   Boys on Rocks about to Dive

What are the boys doing here? How do they feel? Are there any differences between the ways individual boys feel? How did they get there? Have pupils ever been in a similar situation? How did they feel?

Written work: Imagine that you are one of the boys in the photograph — How did you get there? What does it feel like now? What happened after the photograph was taken?

### 7   Return to Air

The experience described here — and described in a language with which pupils will easily identify — makes a good starting point for discussing many activities which have an important element of adventure, and provides a useful (though deceptively simple) model for attempting other descriptions. The aspect of the passage which makes it a good deal more than a description of learning to duck-dive is the way in which Philippa Pearce writes so much of the boy's character into it: an aspect which sensitive readers see — and attempt to bring out, often very successfully, in their own efforts — without having their attention drawn to it. For the less able, a vivid account of actually learning to do something is perhaps enough: the emphasis should be on getting across how it felt.

Possible subjects for writing: learning to swim, to dive, to rock-climb, to ride a horse, to water-ski, to vault (or other gymnastic skills), to ice-skate. But children will come up with their own ideas. (The best work I've had after this came from a girl who wrote about learning to row which didn't seem to me to offer much. I was wrong.)

### 9   Underwater

What is the man doing? How does he feel? What does the expression on his face tell us? Look at his arm and hand: can you imagine how they feel? Have you ever done anything at all like this? When? How did it feel? What happens next?

Imagine that you are the man in the photograph. Describe what you are doing and how you feel. If you have ever been in a situation where you had the same sort of feelings as the man in the photograph, describe it.

### 12   Episode

I hope this 'Episode' can be used in a number of ways: as a starting point for improvised drama in the classroom; as the start of a text of a play which pupils can continue to write either individually or (better, perhaps) in groups and later perform for the rest of the class, or put onto tape as a play for voices; as the starting point of a discussion about the ways in which atmosphere can be created both in classroom drama and taped plays. It is interesting and instructive to follow any such work by listening to and/or reading *Julian* complete: it can be found in *Listening and Writing* (B B C pamphlet, Autumn 1970). Also well worth reading is Ray Jenkins's *Why a Play?* (see pages 39–40).

Connections with the kind of prose fiction children will be reading at this age are not difficult to make; perhaps particularly obvious is the work of Alan Garner ('Episode' is very suggestive of the kind of atmosphere created at the start of *Elidor*, for example, *Other Worlds*, page 52). See also *The Old Man of Mowe* by Alan Garner.

## 16    Freeze Pictures

A sequence of photographs designed to stimulate talk and acting, to give as it were, children a chance to see themselves in action to prompt questions such as: 'What kind of situations are being acted out here?' 'How do we know?' 'What can we learn from facial expression, the use of hands, the ways in which people are standing?' and so on. Most of the situations photographed are clearly about some moment of crisis, some moment in an 'adventure' and as such complement any discussion of 'Episode'. The photographs themselves may suggest ideas for drama; it is more likely however that these will come out of discussion – either of the photographs or of other material in the book which lends itself to dramatic treatment.

Most of the photographs here were taken by Brother Gabriel Barnfield, whose *Creative Drama in Secondary Schools* (Macmillan) contains some stimulating comments on the 'freeze' idea, as well as on the use of creative drama in general.

## 20    The Barn

Like 'Death of a Naturalist', page 36, from Seamus Heaney's volume of the same name (Faber), which contains other poems which some pupils will enjoy reading for themselves, as does Heaney's later volume *Door into the Dark* (Faber). Many of Heaney's poems are about moments of crisis and 'adventure' in childhood and are very accessible to children of eleven and twelve. 'The Barn' is a very good poem to read, discuss and read again – and leave at that. Geoffrey Summerfield in *Topics in English* (Batsford) makes the point that we should not be always using a poem as the starting point, the stimulus, for children's own writing: that we should often be content with the experience of having read and reflected. The poem does, however, lead to pupils thinking about similar experiences they have had, similar places they have known and as such may be the starting point for their own writing, either verse or prose.

## 21    Abbattoir

A photograph which should prompt the obvious: 'What is it?' and lead onto 'Can you imagine how it feels?' and so connect with, and, perhaps, help any consideration of, the very tactile quality of 'The Barn' ('smooth, chilly concrete', 'the zinc burned like an oven', 'cobwebs clogging up your lungs' and so on). I think that in the stimulation of children's writing we often tend to forget the tactile, to concentrate on the visual and auditory.

## 22–3　Day of the Fair

Andrew Wyeth's paintings (there are others on pages 47 and 120) are ideal for this age group: detailed, sensitive to texture, and full of the lives and personalities of his subjects. Wyeth lives in a remote village in New England, painting and re-painting the same people.

It is the day of the fair, and this girl is dressed up for the great occasion. For some reason she has been prevented from going, and Wyeth has caught the mood brilliantly. Notice the facial expression in conjunction with the posture of the hands – distracted, moody, nervously miserable. Are adults ever quite so completely, totally dejected as children can be? It is a dejection that seems to master the whole body.

Children will identify with this picture very readily – why can't she go? When have you felt like this? Before allowing them to strike out from the picture, however, it is worth getting them to think about the picture itself. What does the light tell you about the weather outside? What can you tell from the girl's clothes – the collar on her blouse, the hair-band, etc.? Why did Wyeth show so much of the room she is sitting in?

## 25　Power

A very fine story in its own right but also one which opens up a large area for talk and writing. Pupils' interest in animals and birds at this age is well known but they also have a particular interest in those in some sort of distress – lost, injured, trapped – and most will have had some experiences involving them, which for them are 'adventures', and they will be only too happy to share them, and to write about them.

## 36　Death of a Naturalist　See note on 'The Barn', page 96.

## 38　First Time Solo, Perilous Playground

A couple of photographs which may help discussion of the sensations written about in 'The Tree', page 39.

## 39　The Tree

A situation such as the one written about here will be fairly common to most children of the age group. Most will, at some time or other, have been in a position very similar to that of the boy trapped in the tree and unable to move from sheer fear. Like other extracts in the book, however, it will not have appeared to them to have been as dramatic as the situation here; discussion and prompting can frequently make them see that it was in every way just as dramatic. Two situations common to a lot of children have come to light in my discussions of the passage with children: having to pass down a street, along an alley-way, where there is a particularly frightening dog; and fear of the dark. Tony Connor in his 'St Mark's Cheetham Hill' vividly suggests the kind of sensation that discussion will throw up:

Perhaps a boy delivering papers
in winter darkness before the birds wake,
keeps to Chapel Street's far side, for fear
some corpse interned at his ankle's depth
might shove a hand through the crumbling wall
and grab him in passing; (*With Love Somehow*, OUP).

There are many such situations which children can be helped to think about, helped to remember, to re-live through the mind's eye, ear, hand, nose and tongue ('can you feel *now* what it's like to have a mouth full of dirt?'). Once the incident is clear in the head again the writing — either in verse or prose — will come easily.

The other interesting thing about the passage and about which pupils will want to talk is, of course, the attitudes of the boys. It would be easy to point a moral about the lack of sympathy on the part of Brad and his brother for the unfortunate Theon. Fairly full and free discussion however reveals to them that there is in most of them a bit of both sides: that few people are really quite as timid as Theon, and few quite as bold as Brad and his brother.

An able class, or able pupils, will enjoy William Sansom's *The Vertical Ladder* (Penguin).

### 40    Child Crying

Questions for discussion: 'What is going on here?' 'What has happened to the little boy?' 'How does he feel?' 'How do the others feel?' 'Where do you imagine the photograph was taken?' 'Why are some of the children not wearing shoes?' 'Are the children poor, or not, do you think?'

Suggestion for writing: 'Imagine that you are one of the children in the photograph and write a story in the first person making the situation photographed here the climax — what happened before it, and after it?'

### 46    'Christina's World' by Andrew Wyeth

I imagine that familiarity with the picture and Richardson's comment — familiarity through browsing — makes for a much more sensitive discussion than children coming to it cold and being expected to enter into it quickly.

'What were your first impressions of the picture?' 'Why?' 'Have those impressions been changed since you got to know the picture better?' 'Why?' 'What features of the picture are particularly noticeable?' 'Why do you imagine that they were made so noticeable?' 'What do you imagine it would be like to be Christina?' 'Why do you imagine Andrew Wyeth finds the Olson family and farm so fascinating?'

It is not difficult to get across the notion that 'adventure' is a question of degree — quite often.

### 48    The Bicycle Race

The tension and excitement here will be a tension and excitement familiar to all but the very least sports-minded. The fact that it is cycle racing — a sport very few will actually have taken part in — is of little consequence. A point of entry to discussion of the story is through the bicycle: almost all pupils will have ridden one even if they don't own one, and most will know what it is like to ride a bike until the legs and chest ache. (As one boy wrote: 'I could feel my chest tightening and legs knotting up as I was reading the story'.)

Perhaps the story appeals more readily to boys than to girls but most girls will at least have known the tension in watching a crucial sporting event and the feeling of wanting a particular side to win is strong in most of us.

Reading and discussion of the story can fairly easily lead — perhaps at a later date — into consideration of excitement at any sporting event. In my experience for most boys (and for a larger number of girls than would seem to be recognized) this has generally been football. It is perhaps salutary to get away from the pretty superficial yet nevertheless important blind adulation of 'Chelsea for the cup', 'George Best is the Greatest' to some thinking about how both we and others feel and behave when playing a game or taking part in a race, or watching a team we support. And writing — about a multitude of events and situations — should soon follow.

*Best Sports Stories* edited by Paul Edwards (Faber) is well worth looking at and having to hand for children who are particularly keen on the subject. The introduction seems to me to be especially interesting.

## 56 Goal!

Speaks for itself — or does it?

## 59 Rites

Unlike 'The Bicycle Race', which focuses on a sporting event as it happens, 'Rites' opens up the other great aspect of sport: talking about, exaggerating, exulting in, pre-living, reliving, making comparisons, insisting that players, games, matches, of yesterday were better than those of today, or vice-versa, and so on. Virtually every sport lends itself to glamorization of this sort. Once pupils have got the hang of the language here — not as difficult as at first appears — they soon recognize that Brathwaite has captured something of the universal idiom used for talking-over sporting events: essentially it is the manner they adopt at school on a Monday morning when discussing last Saturday's big match, the manner that they know their fathers adopt in the pub:

I told him over an' over
agen: *watch de ball, man,* watch
de ball like it hook to you eye . . .

Look wha happen las' week at de O
val!

At de Oval?
What happen las' week at de Oval?

You mean to say that you come
in here wid dat lime-skin cone

that you callin' a hat . . .

Apart from the talk about the mystique and glamour of sport which the poem gives rise to, it provides a model for children's own efforts, either in the form of verse or drama: 'The Big Fight', 'The Local Derby', 'The Semi-Final', and so on, where they can have a go at capturing the nuances and idiosyncrasies of their own local language.

## 65 The Little Fishes

The delightful thing about this story is that most first- certainly most second-year pupils are old enough to see what is going on here, and yet are sufficiently near to the age of the boy in the story to remember quite vividly when they half believed there were pike as big as hippopotomassiz, or that there was such a thing as 'neck-oil', or whatever. And they will want to share their memories: first in talk, later in writing. Some of the memories will be of having been taken in by adults (most of whom were quite well meaning really), others will be of having got hold of the wrong end of a stick for some reason.

Those who are particularly interested in the fishing aspect of the story may like to look at *Best Fishing Stories* edited by John Moore (Faber). Also of interest will be the *Fishing* sequence in the B BC *Listening and Writing* pamphlet of Autumn 1969.

Michael Baldwin's *Grandad with Snails* (Hutchinson) provides many points of comparison.

### 73   Strips

It looks difficult to understand, but is it? Once the structure is pointed out, children enter very readily into Morgan's concrete poem: a person or an object, then a situation, followed by a result! Can pupils fill in the 'grammar' of these episodes? What is the situation and why does the result result?

### 74   Comic Strips

These excerpts from comics are included to provide a point of focus for discussion, or thinking about, a source that provides a good deal of various adventure for a significant number of pupils. The curious mixture of fantasy and reality, the very immediate sense of drama, the (to our minds) superficiality, the pictorial representation of sound are all worth talking about with children. I think we should be wary to imply any judgements but we can provide a useful service by getting children to examine their own responses. Complete 'texts' for use with groups will be fairly readily available from members of classes. Interesting drama can often result from an examination of a comic story.

A lot of children are only too ready to try their hand at making a strip. Is there any difference between Roy Lichtenstein's sophisticated parody comic style and the originals on pages 74–7?

### 79   A Mining Man

Jobs which provide an element of adventure presumably hold a fascination for us all: we may not want to do them, but we can't help but wonder at the men who spend their lives fishing the deep seas, working on oil rigs, erecting suspension bridges, even, I suppose, driving long-distance lorries. There is something about such jobs which, we perhaps imagine, more than compensates for the physical danger. Perhaps what seems to be the essential simplicity of struggling against the elements, the comparatively easy measurement of success, is something which appeals to a basic instinct. Whatever it is, at the age of eleven or twelve what used to be a romantic interest in jobs – 'I want to be a fireman, an engine-driver' – has been replaced by a more realistic interest, but some of the romance lingers on and it is not our job to dispel it, but to put it into some sort of perspective.

This passage seems to me to do just that: to confirm the notion that the mine is a place of romance and challenge as well as one of real physical discomfort and danger, but also to suggest that what makes it function are ordinary human qualities – care, courage, determination, sweat, resourcefulness and so on. The graphic details of the passage make for a possibility of identification rather unusual in descriptions of this kind.

The main point for discussion is the kind of man Lister Addy is. It is important here that his good sense, judgement, physical strength, cool-headedness is made as much of as his courage and selflessness; the last paragraphs are important here; most pupils can see it not merely as an indication of self-effacement but also as an indication of the matter-of-fact nature of the job.

A useful and telling exercise is for pupils to re-tell the story as if they were Addy: those who see nothing but danger, drama, excitement in the passage will soon have their notions modified by sensitive first-person accounts by their class-mates. (One girl who wrote such an account was already wondering whether they would have drunk all the tea when she was lifting the tram from Winterbottom! This no doubt means that I had played down the danger and the drama too much in my discussion!)

Most classes will contain children whose fathers or uncles or neighbours do jobs which are adventurous in some way or other. Portable tape-recorders for interviews are useful here. It may even be possible to persuade somebody whose work is (or was) adventurous to speak to a class.

The subject offers a good deal of scope for group work.

Frederick Grice's *Bonnie Pit Laddie* (OUP) may well be the book out of which a consideration of the passage arises. Other useful books are Clancy Segal's *Weekend in Dinlock* (Penguin), Orwell's *Down the Mine* (Collected Essays, Journals and Letters, volume 1, Penguin) and Lawrence's *Sons and Lovers* (Penguin). See also *Things Working,* pages 72–83.

## 90  The Streets of Laredo

Like comics, cowboys and the world that goes with them – as portrayed on television and in films – exert a pretty powerful hold on the imaginations of some pupils (though I suspect less than they used to do). The life of adventure, the hero figure, the simple formula of good against bad provide the pull. The traditional American ballad can, I think, without denying the Wild West its glamour, act as a corrective in providing recognizable human emotions in a situation which is normally without them. Geoffrey Summerfield's section 'The Wild West' in *Topics in English* (Batsford) is particularly helpful when doing follow-up work on the subject.

## 93  The Bear

An important aspect of adventure is hunting, more especially hunting which involves a degree of danger to the hunter. This passage from D. R. Sherman's *Old Mali and the Boy* – to my mind a brilliant story, and one which raises many important and interesting questions, most of which can most profitably be taken up with pupils rather older than first and second year (though I have known a number of second years, mainly girls, read it with enthusiastic interest) – brings home remarkably vividly the moment of the kill. It does it also in such a way that the ethical question of why kill the bear at all is one which does not immediately present itself: somehow the justification is built into the extract.

M. K. Rawlings's *The Yearling* (Peacock) (or abridged – more suitable for class use – Heinemann) contains several episodes concerned with the killing of wild animals and is eminently suitable (for me, indispensable) reading for the age group. See also *Creatures Moving*, especially pages 86–109.

### 100 Found Poem: What to Say to the Pasha

Like Edwin Morgan's 'Strips', this splendid 'found poem' provides a
marvellous framework for pupil's own story-writing. These 'poems' while
often amusing in their own right provide just enough detail of a situation
to start children off on their own, but not so much that their imagination
is hampered.

The 'found poem' could perhaps be used more than it is by English
teachers. Of course, it is *not* poetry, but it does encourage children to be
much more aware of their language environment — to find the funny,
intriguing, bizarre in places where it might not have been noticed before.
In short, it is one, perhaps modest, way of making children more aware
of the world about them. Two anthologies of 'found poems' for the
teacher's interest and reference are published by Kayak: *Pioneers of
Modern Poetry* and *Losers Weepers*.

### 108 Howitt Leads a Rescue March

Adventure at its most grand, perhaps: exploration, particularly exploration
of areas never before visited, and the dangers that go with it. Like André in
'Power' who had seen an Everest film once and for a long time after
imagined he was Hillary or Tensing or both, conquering a mountain, first-
and second-year pupils have a strong interest in such exploits. Whereas
with André, who was ten, the interest is very much at the level of
self-identification, by the age of eleven or, certainly, twelve, such an
interest has developed into a more objective questioning of 'what it was
really like'. With the graphic detail, precise dates and times, the sense of
immediacy, this is what Alan Moorehead provides. Although the episode
here is fairly self-contained, a brief filling in of the background by the
teacher is obviously helpful. More able pupils will want to read the whole
book (*Cooper's Creek* by Alan Moorehead, Hamish Hamilton).
James Vance Marshall's *Walkabout* (Peacock), as well as being a fine
book in its own right, provides a useful service in giving something of
the feel of Australia.

Projects on Australia may well result from a reading of the extract. Again,
Geoffrey Summerfield provides many useful suggestions. If the extract is
developed into an interest in exploration in general, possible subjects for
group or individual studies are: The Arctic, Antarctica, The Sahara,
The Amazon, Great Mountains.

### 120 Legend

To my mind Judith Wright's poem captures the very essence of adventure
which the passages and poems in the book suggest from various angles.
It is a poem which offers a lot to talk about and which children enjoy
discussing; many will also enjoy writing their own 'Legend'.

### 122 Comfort

A neat example, to finish with, of non-adventure: the moment when
stories, like books, end, the satisfaction of danger over and things done
right. But also a reminder that everything is really relative, that everything
is in a sense an adventure: it is just a question of seeing that the storm is
the right size.

# Other Worlds
## Donald Ball and Patrick Radley

The attitudes of M'Choakumchild and Gradgrind are still not unknown in schools today and an anthology which explores fantasy will doubtless still need defending. It is often claimed that writers in English have written very well in the area of fantasy and the search for material for this anthology has amply confirmed this. And certainly, if we choose our material well in the classroom, our pupils will want to talk, write, paint, draw, act. As J. R. R. Tolkien said, 'Successful fantasy produces a secondary world into which both designer and spectator can enter, to the satisfaction of their senses while they are inside.' It is, I think, generally recognized that the world of fantasy plays a very real part in a child's progress to maturity. All children, not just very young children, need some outlet for fantasy, for if their imagination is given shape, they come to terms with it. Helen Cresswell recently suggested that she would like to see a period for day-dreaming on the school timetable. The chances of this happening are pretty remote, but its value to pupils would be enormous. What happens in fantasy for the child is real. It is a way to sort out the fears and solve the problems of daily life. It is through fantasy that a child relates to the world and the things in it, and the things inside himself. It is his way of becoming himself and childhood is the time for becoming.

We can never expect to understand the child's fantasies fully. That would probably be asking too much even of a psychoanalyst. But a psychoanalyst would realize, as teachers must realize, that in the reading of fantasy and the expression of it in art or writing the child is exploring his own inner life. It helps him to understand who he is, to form his values, and, oddly enough, it helps to give him a sense of reality. Therefore, the opportunities for this purposeful kind of fantasy must be nourished by teachers. It is not necessary that we should fully understand, but it is necessary that we should be there to encourage it and create the climate in which it will grow.

It was with the preceding thoughts in mind that the anthology was compiled. It owes much to colleagues who have helped without realizing it, simply by talking informally, especially John Grundy and David Hunt. A lot is owed to my colleagues on the PEP who have provided so many stimulating ideas when we have met, and above all to Martin Lightfoot of Penguin Education for help, guidance and forbearance. I must not, however, forget the greatest debt of all — to my pupils in various schools since 1959, but especially 3A (1962—3) at Welland Park High School, Market Harborough and 3A and its fourth and fifth year manifestations (1967—70) at Moat Boys' School, Leicester.

# Books for the Classroom Library

Kathleen Arnott, *African Myths and Legends* (OUP)

L. M. Boston, *The Children of Green Knowe* (Faber)

Ted Hughes, *The Iron Man* (Faber)

Norton Juster, *The Phantom Tolbooth* (Puffin)

Clive King, *Stig of the Dump* (Puffin)

Madeleine L'Engle, *A Wrinkle in Time* (Longman)

C. S. Lewis, *The Lion, the Witch and the Wardrobe* (Puffin)

J. R. Martin, *Uncle* (Cape)

William Mayne, *Earthfasts* (Hamish Hamilton)

James Reeves, *Prefabulous Animals* (Heinemann)

J. R. R. Tolkien, *The Hobbit* (Allen & Unwin)

T. H. White, *The Book of Beasts* (Cape)

# Notes

### 8    Running Olive Tree

One can often find natural objects which have human characteristics in their appearance, trees especially. Children can be asked if they have seen any such examples themselves and what they can tell about them. They may be able to bring along a few small examples, or a few cuttings from papers and magazines.

Suppose a tree could really walk? And had a brain? We are moving into the realms of science fiction and (most obviously) into the area of *The Day of the Triffids* by John Wyndham (Penguin), to which children of this age may be best introduced by excerpts read aloud.

### 9    Three Riddles

With these examples and any others that can be found – see *The Earliest English Poems* translated by Michael Alexander (Penguin) and *The Battle of Maldon and Other English Poems* by Kevin Crossley-Holland and Bruce Mitchell (Macmillan) – children can be asked to compose their own riddles, or, working in pairs, to produce something like 'Questions and Answers'. *The Lore and Language of School Children* by Iona and Peter Opie (OUP) is a useful source. See also the first ten passages in *Voices* 1, edited by Geoffrey Summerfield (Penguin). There are references to similar passages in *Junior Voices* listed in the *Teachers' Handbook* under 'Riddles and Charms', page 17.

### 10    Problem 1

As the photograph and poem are so closely connected, one may go further than Heather Holden's answer and say what *is* in the parcel. As for **Problem 2** on page **11**, 'What will happen?'

### 12    Ye Tortures

This kind of playing with words which, though nonsense, appears to be sense because they obey grammatical rules has always been popular with children. A poem of a similar kind which gives splendid opportunity for choral speech work, with percussion effects, is C. S. Lewis's 'Narnian Suite'. See *Voices* 1, page 51.

### 13    The Big Lake of Pois-Résine

What sort of an adventure are the riders involved in? What kind of a world is this? Does the rider on the cliff succeed in avoiding capture or death? These are only the first questions!

A group of children might have a very worthwhile time making a tape recording to accompany the picture.

**14—17  Sounds**

Children enjoy inventing words in this sort of way. For further examples
see the book itself — *Ounce Dice Trice* by Alastair Reid (Dent).

**18  Cardinal Ideograms**

Some discussion of this poem may be useful to share different reactions to
the shapes of the numbers. Alternatives may be considered for the same
figures, or interpretations of the same figure done in a different
typographical style, or the poem may be continued to twenty. The
letters of the alphabet could be treated. In this connection counting
words are also of interest, see *Voices* 1, pages 14 and 15.

**19  Butterfly**

Why does he cry at the end? Perhaps children could be asked to write their
version of his writing on the paper. A group could probably work out a
similar sequence of drawings.

**20—21  The Secret in the Cat**

Children enjoy making animals out of unusual materials. Groups could
make an animal and compose a poem to go with it, or perhaps improvise
a scene in which it was the central feature.

**22—3  They have yarns**

Children are often artists in this kind of exaggeration, and will enjoy telling
tall stories they have heard or making them up on the spot.

See in this connection 'The Derby Ram' (*Voices* 1, page 31). For further
ideas in relation to this whole area and beyond it, see *Topics in English* by
Geoffrey Summerfield (Batsford), pages 76—8.

**24  The Far-Famed Fairy Tale of Fenella**

This *tour-de-force* on the letter F could well serve as a basis for imitation.
It needs also to be read aloud!

**25  Sale by Auction**

Humour of this kind is very popular with children. Again they are good at
it themselves often, and can be asked to collect as many examples of it as
they can find. Advertisements offer a fruitful form for the expression of
these discoveries.

**26—7  The Stunning Great Meat Pie**

Another example of the tall story referred to above. See also for a different
kind, equally tall, *Ventures*, pages 64—70.

**29—30  Traveller's Tales**

The *Traveller's Tales* are in fact a forgery. They were not written by Sir
John Mandeville, but were probably compiled from various sources by
Jean d'Outrenense, a writer of histories and fables, in the second part of the
fourteenth century. According to d'Outrenense, Sir John Mandeville took
the name Jehan Bourgogne or Jean à la Barbe and died in 1382 in France.

Discussion could well concentrate on what could lead people to believe in this kind of nonsense. Those with a taste for looking things up may well search out other accounts of early voyages and of the inhabitants of far off places. Others may like to set about inventing equally good forgeries, brought up to date, or set in an earlier century.

### 32–3   Moon People

A very early example of Science Fiction. It appears to make Lucian the ancestor of H. G. Wells's *The First Men in the Moon* (Collins) which can be introduced at this point. Indeed a whole range of S.F. may appear at this stage so long as it is borne in mind that much good writing of that kind is very adult and is often approachable only by children older than those who are likely to be using this book. Science Fact can also be linked with this and the work broadened out to a treatment of space generally.

For ideas about work in this area see the notes referring to pages 110 to 118 of *Things Working* in the Handbook.

*Other Sources*

Music
*The Planets* by Gustav Holst.
*The Rite of Spring* by Stravinsky.
*Also Sprach Zarathustra* by Richard Strauss.

Poems
'Silver' by Walter de la Mare.
'Tea in a Space Ship' by James Kirkup.
'Expanding Universe' by Norman Nicholson.
'The Moon' by W. H. Davies.
Ted Hughes's Moon poems, an example of which is to be found on page 35.
'Star Talk' by Robert Graves.

Prose
*The Time Machine* by H. G. Wells (Heinemann).
*Islands in the Sky* by A. C. Clarke (Digit).
*The Boy's Book of Space* by Patrick Moore is a good factual book, though somewhat outdated now.
*The Death of Metal* by Donald Suddaby (OUP).

### 39–42   The Making of the Drum

The poem lends itself to choral speaking and could well lead to experiments in drum rhythms on the desks or with percussion instruments on loan from the Music Department. In fact, with the cooperation of a sympathetic music teacher it would be possible to work out a musical setting of the poem. For an idea of how this could be done Lewis Carroll's 'Jabberwocky' on the Argo record (DA91) accompanying *Voices* 1 may be of use with the related notes.

### 44   The Making of a Monster

Found poems can have a place in the classroom. The example given here, with an explanation of what a 'found' poem is, could set the children off on their own search. See *Things Working*, pages 71 and 94, *Creatures Moving*, pages 12–13, and *Ventures*, pages 100–105 for other found poems. See note on these earlier in the Handbook.

### 47 Mr Beale

This might well start an account of eccentric characters known or invented. Or could form the point of departure for improvised drama groups acting sections of this story or launching out into scenes about other eccentrics.

### 52–61 The Old Blind Fiddler

Stories about leaving the real world behind and stepping out into a fantasy world are fairly common. Under this heading come, for instance, the C. S. Lewis's 'Narnia' Books (Puffin), the thirteen 'Oz' books of Frank L. Baum (a most remarkable series), *Tom's Midnight Garden* by Philippa Pearce (OUP). Children can invent their own new land and the notes to page 118 of *Things Working* show what can happen when such an invention succeeds.

### 62–3 Earth Orbit

A passage illustrative of the way in which children can become completely involved in their own fantasy and of how easily it can be broken by the mundane intervention of the adult. Children can be asked to tell about some such episode in their own lives. Does the illustration bring the experience back, or could it be a pointer to regaining the experience? What have they used boxes for in similar situations?

### 65 I Dreamed I Was

What do you dream about? Other dreams could be Robert Graves, 'What Did I Dream?', Robert Frost, 'Nocturnes', 'Acquainted with the Night', Edward Thomas, 'Cock-Crow', 'Lights Out'. Dream material gives opportunity for hilarious and worthwhile group drama work.
See also for suggestions about further material and ideas pages 86 to 88 of *Topics in English* by Geoffrey Summerfield (Batsford).

### 66 The Loch Ness Monster's Song

This needs to be said aloud: perhaps a tape-recorder can provide controlled conditions under which that can take place! Also efforts in the same medium can be made, and similarly taped. Best, perhaps, after a scrutiny of other Morgan poems — and there are a number in PEP Stage One Books. The Loch Ness Monster itself can be pursued — what is it? Or he? Is there really a monster? And what about prehistoric monsters in general? The 'Tyrannosaurus Rex' extract by Ray Bradbury on page 68 and the photograph on pages 68 and 69 can be considered here. See, too, the description of the creatures from Mars in H. G. Wells's *The War of the Worlds* (Heinemann), and also Nigel Kneale's *Quatermass and the Pit* (Penguin). The work could well be divided, in fact, between fact regarding prehistoric monsters, research into the Loch Ness Monster story, and S.F. original writing. Two stories which are worth consideration along with the Loch Ness Monster are *The Spanish Cave* by Geoffrey Household (Puffin) and the short story by Ray Bradbury 'The Foghorn' from *Golden Apples of the Sun* (Corgi).

### 70–77 The One Who Waits

A fine story, very well paced by Ray Bradbury. It would make a very good radio play, with suitable music. Different groups in a class can each be set this task, the results taped, and finally performed to all and discussed.

**78  Under a Ramshackle Rainbow**

Desolation and horror. Man of less importance than a malevolent nature. How do children see this? This is an area in which their responses are unpredictable and often very strong: and they need to be given scope for whatever expression they can give to the feelings and ideas raised.

**80, 81  Gnaw short the long nose, Resurrection Song**

The comments made above apply even more sharply here, perhaps.

**82–3  The Legend of Alderley**

'Here they lie in enchanted sleep until . . . England shall be in direst peril. . . . Then out from the hill these must ride and . . . drive the enemy into the sea.' Children can be asked to imagine that such a peril has come, and make it the basis for story-writing or group improvised drama. (This is probably a place for other of Alan Garner's books to be recommended and talked about, perhaps read in extract to whet some appetites.)

**84–7  Death a Prisoner**

Splendid chance for controlled group acting, to express as fully as they can what the story tells. Another story about Death which gives a similar opportunity is the Robbers' Story from the middle of *The Pardoner's Tale*, in Nevill Coghill's Penguin Chaucer.

**89–92  The Fight**

If children wish to read more of *Beowulf*, the version by Rosemary Sutcliffe (Puffin) can confidently be recommended.
At the end of the extract, Grendel returns to his home beneath the sea to die. His situation and his feelings can well be discussed and serve as the material for follow-up work.

**92  Wodwo**

Groups in the class will produce different versions of what Wodwo is, or different drawings. Or they may decide in their minds, act out the 'thing's' actions, and then get us to guess what it is. Similarly about the picture.

**95–8  Heartless Beauty**

The story is very clear in outline, the characters are straightforward, and it has a repetitive pattern. It would adapt very well into a play – for radio, scripted, with sound effects and music; or it could be interpreted freely in an improvised drama situation. This story is quoted in Peter Aston and John Paynter, *Sound and Silence: Classroom Projects in Creative Music* (CUP), a book which ought ideally be on every English Teacher's shelf. It contains many suggestions for creative music, and is perhaps specially relevant to *Other Worlds*.

**100  To Make a Play**

Do they feel this when they have made a play? Or when they have watched others making one? To test the point it may be sufficient to set about some group drama on the spot, to work on it until they get the feel of involvement, from inside and from without, and then try out the poem. If the poem seems wrong, is it the play that's not good enough? Or do plays do other quite different things to you?

## Reading

For advice on reading and lists of books in this rich area Margery Fisher's 'critical appraisal of modern fiction for children', *Intent upon Reading* (Brockhampton Press), remains basic, especially chapters 5, 6, 7 and 8 and their concluding Reading Lists. This book, written in 1961, was revised in 1964, and the final chapter in the later edition looks at books published between those dates and lists them under headings including *Fantasy* and *Myths, Legends, Folk and Fairy-Tales, and some modern analogues.* Brockhampton Press followed these books in 1970 with a paperback Handbook for Librarians entitled *Children's Fiction* by Sheila G. Ray. Though this does not include lists, and covers a wide range of specialized topics, it refers in the text to a great number of good books, and chapters 2, 3 and 7 are especially relevant in connection with *Other Worlds*.

# I Took my Mind a Walk
## Patrick Radley and George Sanders

*I Took my Mind a Walk* has a less specific subject matter than the other titles in Stage One of the Penguin English Project. Moreover, for many children it is breaking new ground: it cannot draw widely on previous experience but must make its own going, create its own starting points. Most children seem to take for granted the overall setting of their immediate and intense concerns within the family or in school. Interest in animals may be for some of them a first lead out into the wider environment, but few at eleven years will have reached any conscious awareness of themselves in relation to their surroundings. Nevertheless, the way to this is the natural one of curiosity and attraction to whatever is lively that functions in any situation. It is an area of growth that we ignore at our peril, for alert response to what surrounds us becomes a condition of self-discovery.

The book's starting point is Norman MacCaig's poem: 'how ordinary/ Extraordinary things are or/How extraordinary ordinary/Things are, like the nature of the mind/And the process of observing'. In so far as the book as a whole is 'about' anything, it concerns the ways in which human beings *figure* their environment to themselves, the way they see and the way they respond to things around them. It opens with the *processes* by which people do this, 'I took my mind a walk/Or my mind took me a walk': predominantly the process of observing, but also of ordering, establishing relationships and likenesses.

Beyond this section, and extending it, is a group of passages centering on the urban environment in which most of our pupils must live and find interest and excitement. It is not easy to find good material of this kind; for most of us, as apparently for most writers, the city still appears to be an environment of convenience, tolerated but never loved, used but not admired. This is, surely, a pity: cities are, after all, where most of us choose to live, and we all acknowledge informally to each other that there are substantial pleasures in city living. More especially, it is a pity for children, who usually lack our prejudices and nostalgias, and to whom we can pass on little language to talk about cities, precious little framework in which to understand and respond to them, and almost no sense of fascination or of possibilities. Perhaps, if the cities survive their own pollution, the next generation can begin to create their own culture of cities.

There follows a section on weather and seasons, which includes within it a range of scene, mood and response. Children of this age are often more influenced and more fascinated by changing weathers and seasons than we adults; or certainly more fascinated than we give them credit for. Perhaps we too easily forget that there is a sense in which each new season for young children is quite a new event, greeting them a year later with different sensations, different interest, so relatively rapid is their development; and the twelve year old still retains this freshness of response.

The book then moves on to more extreme forms of weather and to totally unfamiliar or alien environments. In doing so it makes demands on the imagination, requiring from the reader a mental leap to situations completely outside the range of his experience. Much of this material could well be used in conjunction with schemes in geography and environmental studies, subjects which perhaps too often risk estrangement by disallowing the possible affective aspects of our own and other environments.

In the notes that follow are comments, suggested activities and references, to help the teacher follow up varied responses to the passages. But they may be wide of the mark: we have to be careful that our categories don't falsify the children's responses. For that reason, and also because the book is breaking new ground, activities ought often to come first and consideration of the passages second. Shared practical experience is the right rich ground for these passages to fall on, so long as the activities are real and relevant. It follows naturally, therefore, that teachers using the book should be urged to do one thing above all; namely, to take the children *out* of the school, into the immediate environment of city, town or village, and further afield. In a phrase, to take their minds a walk.

# Books for the Classroom Library

Kenneth Allsop, *Fit to Live In?* (Penguin)

Sheila Tidmarsh, *Disaster* (Penguin)

Frank W. Lane, *The Elements Rage* (David & Charles)

Folco Quilici, *The Great Deserts* (Collins)

Maurice Herzog, *Annapurna* (Cape)

Michael Baldwin, *Grandad with Snails* (Hutchinson)

Marjorie Kinnon Rawlings, *The Yearling* (Peacock)

Andrew Salkey, *Earthquake* (OUP)

A. Rutgers van der Loeff, *Avalanche* (Puffin)

Laura Ingalls Wilder, *The Long Winter* (Puffin)

Jean George, *My Side of the Mountain* (Puffin)

Paul Berna, *Flood Warning* (Puffin)

# Notes

**8   Detroit 1941**

The picture lends itself to being looked at any way up. Do we have to know what it is of to enjoy it? Are there different ways of seeing it?

Are there any Japanese or Chinese prints available in school for comparison here?

**9   An Ordinary Day**

This poem can well be made the excuse for a simple piece of work on perception, on 'the process of observing', on how the mind takes a part in making what we see.

As one illustration of 'the nature of the mind' optical illusions can be examined (for an example, see *Ventures*, page 71). One way of doing this is to project images, say a varied selection of transparencies, onto a surface that distorts and then set beside them undistorted objects. Distorting agencies include folding screens or textured surfaces: the bigger the image the better — it's worth getting hold of a 65mm lens rather than the standard 35. Or a tape-recorder can be used to show how much we 'cut out' in hearing. A 'happening' can be improvised: for example, a street accident can be devised in detail and then acted, or with the cooperation of another teacher or a group from another form, an apparently serious and shocking interruption to the lesson can be arranged! These can be discussed directly they have occurred and details compared. How many came in? What did they want? Who pushed all the books over? Or detailed accounts can be written-up, complete with plans, and compared at length. The evident discrepancies and differences provide interesting evidence for a discussion about perception!

*Other Sources*

*Eye and Brain* by R. L. Gregory (Weidenfeld & Nicolson).
*The Psychology of Perception* by M. D. Vernon (Penguin).
*The Graphic Work of M. C. Escher* (Oldbourne Press).
Bridget Riley's work (for an example, see *Voices*, volume 2, page 35, Penguin).
Moiré patterns.

Part of such a project could be the use of a polaroid camera by a group of children in photographing familiar objects seen from an unfamiliar point of view or in an unfamiliar context, and a quiz run for the whole class when the photographs are finally displayed. Or children can be set the task of taking a whole film in a limited area, say the playground: in this situation the problems of finding a new angle or a view of interest will encourage close looking! (Warning! Photography can be expensive, but need not be unduly so. Consult with someone who knows!)

For the extraordinary in the ordinary, see also *Creatures Moving,* page 22, on microscopic creatures.

A children's book that centres round experiences of heightened perception is Penelope Farmer's *The Magic Stone* (Chatto & Windus). See especially pages 46–8 and 135–8.

Useful work in connection with this poem may be done on a selection of ordinary processes, e.g. the raising of an arm, and something of the extraordinary complexity behind the operation revealed.

10 **Artist's Notebook**

The artist as observer. He shows, in his notes, that he is fascinated by the process of motion, its inevitability, and also by the intrinsic vitality of all kinds of phenomena: wave-mass, water-drop, raindrop, bird, dragonfly, leaf. But he is concerned also with relationship: i.e. of wave shape and falling hair, of the human eye to the sun to the rain in the 'registering' of a rainbow. Throughout the notebooks, comments and drawings complement one another in the process of observation. (It is interesting to see a parallel example of this process in the drawings of the poet Hopkins; see *The Journals and Papers of Gerard Manley Hopkins* edited by Humphry House (OUP) with John Piper's comments on the drawings.)

There is no reason why the obvious should not be done and the extract used as a model for the production of notebooks with similar aims in mind. Instead of drawings, camera or tape-recorder may be used for illustration. For instance, there is scope in simply recording and describing bird song, its shape, tone and quality, and the conditions in which it occurred: here tape-recording and notes will complement one another. If live recording is difficult to obtain – though there should be no difficulty since the simplest of equipment will register sparrows and starlings, and much may be learned about the nature of the environment during the process of getting a clear recording! – a record may be used: recommended, *A Tapestry of Bird Song* (HMV CLP 1723), from which extracts may be taken as wished. Or Leonardo's comments on tree-rings or on water may be taken up and evidence collected to support or disprove what he has said. For this latter purpose simple experiments with water are easy to set up in the classroom using household objects; see *Forms of Energy* (Natural Science, an Integrated Course for Schools, Unit G, Pergamon Press), pages 21–36.

Leonardo's comments on flight can set going a major investigation.

Book sources include
A chapter on bird flight on pages 8 and 9 in *Bird Life* by N. Tinbergen (OUP).
*Wings: Insects, Birds, Men* by Blanche Stillson (Gollancz). Chapter 18 is devoted to the work of Leonardo in trying to perfect a flying machine.
*Things Working,* page 27, shows Leonardo's ideas for a helicopter.
Film material is available from The Royal Society for the Protection of Birds, The Lodge, Sandy, Bedfordshire.
Their Educational Aids Catalogue contains other material relevant to this book.

There is a whole area of study in connection with the artist's particular vision, an area obviously best tackled in cooperation with an artist on the staff. Such study can be set going by the children bringing from home drawings by their younger brothers and sisters. Or a group can draw or paint part of the room, which can then be photographed, and the different versions set out for comparison. In this connection the following fully illustrated books are recommended:

*The World through Blunted Sight* by Patrick Trevor-Roper (Thames & Hudson).

*Vasarely* by Victor Vasarely (Neuchâtel: Editions du Griffon).

*Claes Oldenburg* (Tate Exhibition Catalogue, Arts Council of Great Britain).

For a completely different view of water from Leonardo's in the notebooks, see the superb photographs on pages 25–9 in

*Form in Nature and Life* by Andreas Feininger (Thames & Hudson).

## 18–19  Observation

There are contrasts in this poem between 'focusing my attention' and 'staring so fixedly/at nothing', between 'vague, abstracted' and 'awake, absorbed'. Is the observer in a daydream? What sort of absorption does a daydream demand? How much is being 'awake' related to the observer's ability to describe and name the things he's observing? In the extract on page 47 entitled 'Lazying Downriver' Huck Finn notices the life around him in great detail. What sort of 'lazying' is this?

The poem and the picture focus 'on a very small area', look at minutiae minutely! Children enjoy doing this and write well about what they see, with or without a lens, on desk lids, on the hairs on the back of a hand, among the fluff in a corner of a room or in a pocket. This poem by a twelve-year-old girl is a good example:

**A Turned-Over Stone**

Under the darkness
And coldness
A spider lives
His black life,
And as I lift
Up the stone
The life underneath
Scurries away
Out of the
Blinding sunshine
Back into the darkness.

See also Robert Frost's poem 'A Considerable Speck' in *Complete Poems* (Cape).

The relationship between the objective and the subjective in our experience is central to two of the stories in this book. 'Lost in the Desert' (page 97) and 'A Slave becomes a Runaway' (page 112). Nevertheless, this poem, the Leonardo pages and the first poem, along with the illustrations, could make a convenient study unit on Observation.

## 20  The Wildlife of New York City

This long extract from Jack Couffer's book may well need a certain amount of interpretation by the teacher. For instance, there is a good deal of factual information about birds of prey, there are the contrasts in observation of large and small fauna, and there are the implicit comparisons of city blocks and rocky hill country in phrases like 'the cliffs and canyons of the city' and 'the concrete cliffs and asphalt meadows'. There is also the interesting contrast between the two characters: Martin experiences the wild life to a great extent through his camera and looks for explanations of what he sees, while Archie relies only on his own senses and interprets in terms of feeling.

There is obviously wide scope for follow-up work, centred, one would hope, in the practical experience of searching in town or city for signs of wild life and for evidence of the way wild life adapts to man's artificial environment. This can be done by children individually or in groups, with camera, tape-recorder or notebook, and can take its start in the 'hide-outs' and playing grounds that are familiar to them.

A particular element of the extract which can lead to work rooted in their own interests is the discovery of a 'treasure', the arrowhead. Most children have made some such special discovery. How did they find it? When? Where? What did it 'mean'? Is there, perhaps, a story to be told, or invented, about it; a lead into the history of an environment?

Similarly, the phrase about the fish, 'one of the few that still run the gauntlet of pollution between the sea and the upper river', lays open a whole area of study. A project can be set up in which evidence of pollution is collected and set out, emphasis being primarily on the facts rather than on the issues.

*Other Sources*

Particularly useful for the teacher in providing ideas and in giving information about source material are three books in the Penguin Education *Connexions* Series, with the related *Teachers' Guide:*
*Living Tomorrow* by Nigel Calder.
*Disaster* by Sheila Tidmarsh.
*Fit to Live In?* by Kenneth Allsop.
*The Environmental Handbook* edited by John Barr (Ballantine Books in association with Pan Books). See especially 'Part Three: Action Guide', with its comprehensive list of sources in an Appendix, including Films and Film Distributors.
The three volumes in *Interdependence in Nature Series* (Aldus Books). These are splendidly illustrated, but the text is advanced:
*Man's Impact on Nature* by J. A. Lauwerys.
*Conservation* by Joyce Joffe.
*Nature's Network* by Keith Reid.
*The Silent Spring* by Rachel Carson (Penguin).
Closely relevant is an article in *Your Environment* for Spring 1971, volume 2, no. 1, on urban ecology entitled 'Birds in Towns'.
A film not mentioned in *The Environmental Handbook* is 'The Shadow of Progress' made as part of BP's contribution to European Conservation Year. Available from Petroleum Films Bureau, 4 Brook Street, London W1Y 2AY (tel. 01-493 3333).

The description of the peregrine obviously leads into an inquiry into the birds of prey. Sources for such an inquiry include:
*The Peregrine* by J. A. Baker (Penguin).
*A Kestrel for a Knave* by Barry Hines (Penguin).
*The Goshawk* by T. H. White (Penguin).
*My Side of the Mountain* by Jean George (Puffin). A New York boy runs away and lives in the wilderness — and tames a kestrel.

*The Noble Hawks* by N. M. Williams (Chatto & Windus).
There are two Falconry Centres from which material is available, and possibly a visiting lecturer with live birds for a fee: The Falconry Centre, Newent, Glos. and Chilham Castle Falconry Centre, near Canterbury, Kent.

Available from the Royal Society for the Protection of Birds (address given above) is the film *Operation Osprey*, well worth showing in this connection.

## 34 Glasgow and Salford

Two selections from MacColl's and Behan's Topic record, *Streets of Song* (Topic 12T41).

The extract is about how people make an environment their own, using its particular quality for their own purposes. Behind the 'bleakness' there seems to be a keen imaginative activity belying the apparently crippling power of the surroundings.

Here the people worked: a fascinating list of occupations. How does it compare with the children's own locality?

Here the children played: a more typical list. Would they make the same sort of list? What did they do?, and where did they go?
See also section on games in *Family and School*, page 45 of the Handbook.
Other Topic records include:
*Along the Coaly Tyne* (12T189).
*Steam Whistle Ballads* (12T104).
Also traditional material from the London scene on
*Sweet Thames Flow Softly* (Argo DA46) and
*A Merry Progress to London* (Argo DA47), both sung by The Critics.
Relevant films include:
*We are the Lambeth Boys*.
*Our High Street*.
*Bicycle Thieves* (there is a ten-minute clip available).
*Les Jeux Interdits*.
*The Kidnappers*.
*The Red Balloon*.
*Los Olvidados*.
For details see British Film Institute Catalogue, available from The B.F.I., 81 Dean Street, London W1.

Among possible books are
*Where did you go? Out. What did you do? Nothing.*
*What to do by yourself.*
*And another thing*, all by Robert Paul Smith (The World's Work).
*Grandad with Snails* by Michael Baldwin (Hutchinson).
*There is a Happy Land* by Keith Waterhouse (Penguin).
*The Penny World* by Arthur Bantam (Hutchinson).
*Mrs Beer's House* by Patricia Beer (Macmillan).
A possible source of interesting material – and a potentially useful contact in many ways – would be the nearest local radio station.

## 37 Car Fights Cat

A cat's eye view of a car in the urban scene.

Domesticated animals are at the other end of the spectrum from Couffer's peregrine: in the middle come the vermin (page 27) 'that are so much a part of man's ultimate habitat that they are dependent upon it'. The health department in the town hall is a likely source for information on these latter: a rodent officer might be glad to come and give a talk!

*A Kid for Two Farthings* by Wolf Mankowitz (Heinemann) centres round a boy's relationship with a pet and is set in the East End of London.

### 38, 39, 40, 41   Between Walls, The Winter Afternoon, Thames Scene, Hats, People Who Must

Moments, moods, people, things, surroundings, atmosphere and above all the feelings they evoke: creative reactions to the urban scene encapsulated in poetry. A way of following up these little poems is to get the children to make scrap books of just such 'observations', not necessarily in poetry. This may be left to develop by itself over the course of a few weeks, to be completed with drawings or collage. The material may be gathered on the way to and from school, and should aim to have the same 'sharpness' as the poems.

*The People, Yes* by Sandburg is full of varied comments on the relationship between people and their environment, though not always easy to isolate in this long, rambling free-verse epic.
John Schlesinger's *Terminus* is a film which evokes an aspect of the city: as are some of the films mentioned above.
The archives of the local newspaper office might well turn out to be a source of interesting and stimulating pictures of the locality.

### 40–41   New York

Can the photograph be taken in from one position? Or does it have to be moved and seen from different angles? How is it taken? What is a fish-eye lens?

See *Photography and Architecture* by Eric de Maré (Architectural Press). Especially pages 188–9 for an explanation of this picture. (The book is full of evocative photographs of buildings: look, for example, at the Architecture by Accident pictures on pages 168–9.)

### 42   Once at Piertarvit

This poem provides its own unique space by short lines and long stanzas: a good form, perhaps, for a narrative which relates a brief sea-coast incident. We are 'taken along' almost graphically. The 'wonder' concerning the extraordinary event has provoked a clearness of remembering. It is believable because the apple is 'hard and brown', all the people are deliberately named, and the sky is first 'stippled', then 'curdled'. Happening, place, people, gull, all become one.

Surely a poem for thought, some discussion perhaps, but not for dissection? It should 'work'; and could well be a suitable model if poetry-writing is envisaged at some stage.
It forms a fitting introduction to the next six extracts in which description and reflection interact, from the largely reflective 'Lackaday' to the entirely descriptive 'The Beach'.

### 43   Lackaday

Isn't this the sort of feeling that is often a prelude to some adventure? 'And then someone had the idea of . . .'.

## 45 Sunday Afternoons

As with 'Once at Piertarvit' we are made aware of a total situation in which people reflect environment and environment people. But in place of the sense of wonder in that poem there is here a feeling for the bored, lonely and homeless.

A way into this is to ask children to consider how they connect particular people with particular places. Grandparents, aunts and uncles, people met on holiday or at the fair, or the man in the corner shop.

Though the emotional range of this poem may be beyond the scope of some of the children in this age group, it can lead out, and its mixture of facts and feelings provokes responses based closely on their own experience: as in the following poem by a thirteen-year-old girl:

### Hot Chestnuts

Across the bridge, past the cafe,
Sits Ol' Ma Perkins, selling chestnuts,
Popping, warm, brown chestnuts,
Warming, on a cold day
When your breath burns to mist,
And you breathe like a fiery dragon.

The warm fire by which she sits
Glows red in the gloom of the foggy, smoky river,
The wharves nearby look dark and miserable,
And people hurry past in the rain,
But she still sits, there on the bridge,
The gaslights lit, that could be seen reflecting
On the wet shiny pavement,
She still sits
Hoping that someone will buy her hot chestnuts.

You buy some for a shilling,
'Ta very much', she says in a cracked old voice.
Then you walk away,
Carrying the chestnuts
Warm in your hand
The only reminder of her,
She who sat on the bridge
Selling chestnuts, in the rain.

(In fact this poem is an example of the mixture of influences working in the production of a piece of writing. Its immediate 'cause' was the experience of hearing read by the teacher Hemingway's story 'In Another Country' from *Men without Women*. A powerful piece of writing has stimulated imaginative involvement of a kind that has allowed for this resultant mixture in which the story, memories, personal feelings and what is imagined, mingle in a new valid whole.)

## 44—5 Shadow of Mother and Pram

The subject of the photograph contrasts sharply with the content of the poem, family relationship over against homelessness. Yet the distortion is disturbing: is it in the eye of the person looking? For contrast see pages 26—7, 32—3 in *Family and School*. It is possible to produce effective pictures by photographing in a surface which distorts by reflection, e.g. a polished car door. See, in the context of this poem and picture, Truffaut's film, *Les Quatre Cent Coups*.

This passage, read aloud well, draws children in powerfully and allows them to become imaginatively involved with Huck and Jim, or to be 'lazying' in their own situation. Its power lies in its evocation of a totally relaxed frame of mind onto which the surroundings can imprint themselves in detail and be absorbed.

In this case 'listening to the stillness' includes allowing it to happen and recording it. These two activities give scope for experiences different in kind from the Leonardo notebooks, since those include the attempt to understand why things function as they do and the search for relationship between phenomena. Children need opportunities to experience all these different ways of reacting to their surroundings: the recording will probably take place only in the school situation, but it is likely that the initial experience also may need to be provided, outside in the local environment but within the school context.

Do you have to be a particular sort of person to react as Huck reacts? Or in a particular mood? Can Jim be as relaxed as Huck? The questions take us into the book, and may lead to consideration of other extracts from it, e.g. the moment when Huck deceives the two roughs in order to save Jim, or the whole passage in which Huck tricks Jim and finally asks his forgiveness. Obviously the book is a classic source if any work is going to be done on slavery in connection with the passage on pages 112−19. But, as a whole, it is too difficult for most children at this stage. Incidentally, Huck is 'talking' his reminiscences, and similar experiences can be talked down onto tape, or dramatized with taped sound effects: or they may simply be written up in diary form.

A fine description of relaxing, and observing, during a time of great heat occurs in Henri Bosco's *The Fox in the Island* (OUP), pages 74−8.

**49, 50   Wonder Wander, A Sunny Day, The Beach, Waking from a Nap on the Beach**

Four poems which illustrate widely differing uses of free verse: in this respect, potentially helpful in a poetry workshop situation. But how 'free' is the apparently shapeless 'Wonder Wander' and how 'predictable' is May Swenson's poem?

'Wonder Wander' offers scope as a jumping-off ground for a situation, or a happening. It can be dramatized, mimed to the spoken poem as background or interpreted with sound effects and different voices. If a cine camera is available and the necessary small amount of practical knowledge to introduce children to its use, the vitality of this and of the Reznikoff poem asks to be interpreted or paralleled in moving photographic form. What is to be avoided is any attempt to interpret literally. The brief might be simply to go out and photograph what you see next. Just as the images in the two poems may well have been rearranged, so in the film there would be an 'artistic' process of editing.

See *Film Making in Schools* by Douglas Lowndes (Batsford) for full help. The violent juxtaposition of apparently unrelated experiences that is found in 'Waking from a Nap on the Beach' occurs in another form in this stanza from a Lawrence poem:

The spring as it comes bursts up in bonfires green,
Wild puffing of green-fire trees, and flame-green bushes,
Thorn-blossom lifting in wreaths of smoke between
Where the wood fumes up, and the flickering, watery rushes.

Such juxtapositions are not strange to children, as this poem by a twelve-year-old girl shows:

### The Chrysanthemums

Like embers they smoulder,
bloom and burst into fire.
Head like the sun,
alone in a straggling briar.

A monarch among peasants,
petals like rubies:
Stem the shade of emerald,
shining through black patches.

The chrysanthemum perishes,
when rain and cold winds blow:
Black wire thickets thrive
and the bright fire ends its glow.

53—73   The Lawrence passage sets the scene for this section in which violence of the elements is the theme. The key phrase is 'one forgets the rest of life'. Hurricane, tornado, earthquake, flood, extreme cold, each creates a 'massive violent world' in which people are lost in fear. Release comes only after the event, through mutual help, and humour.

It is unlikely that most of our children will have had any experience of the more violent of the elements. It remains important, however, that such experience as they have had of ugly weather should be recalled and used in some way. Straightforwardly this could mean re-enacting somehow an event that was horrifying to them. A good example of a piece of writing that might encourage recall of this sort is in Meindert DeJong's *Hurry Home, Candy* (Lutterworth), pages 62—75, in which the effect of a bad thunderstorm on a family outing is vividly told.

The following extracts about storms from children's fiction are of a similar kind, the first two telling comparable stories about the relief afforded by torrential rain after great heat.

*Thimble Summer* by Elizabeth Enright (Puffin), the first few pages of the book.
*On the Banks of Plum Creek* by Laura Ingalls Wilder (Puffin), pages 144—7.
*Snow-Cloud Stallion* by Gerald Raftery (Puffin), chapters 12 and 13.
*Tom's Midnight Garden* by Philippa Pearce (OUP), pages 52—4.
Two powerful poems about storms are
A sonnet by John Clare entitled 'The Hailstorm in June 1831', from *The Poems of John Clare*, volume 2, edited by J. W. Tibble (Dent), page 138.
'Storm in the Black Forest' by D. H. Lawrence.

On Wind see also:
'There came a Wind' by Emily Dickinson.
*Poetry in the Making* by Ted Hughes (Faber), the chapter on 'Wind and

Weather'. The book is a collection of *Listening and Writing* programmes that the poet compiled for the B B C. The particular chapter includes the following poems:

'Wind' by Ted Hughes.
'The Storm' by Theodore Roethke.
Two untitled poems by Emily Dickinson, the first on the gust of wind before a storm, the second on a cloud-burst.
'After Rain' by Edward Thomas.
'Mists' by Peter Redgrove.
'Winter-Piece' by Charles Tomlinson.
'Teledreamy' by Peter Redgrove.
There is a remarkable piece of film of the break-up of the Tacoma Suspension Bridge, USA, in gale-force winds.
For further material and ideas about possible work on this area of storms, see *Topics in English* by Geoffrey Summerfield (Batsford), pages 62–5.

### 54   Rare Weather, Seasons

This kind of material offers a real challenge to children, to try out their own hyperboles, and tape them in appropriate accents!

### 55   The Rain in Spain

A poem that seems to have emerged from the barometer, the poet is so out of sorts with himself and the weather!

Surely an opportunity for a Wet Afternoon Blues, or mood poetry based on miserable weather! Louis MacNeice's poem 'Glass Falling' is relevant here: Auden's 'Song' ('Stop all the clocks, cut off the telephone . . .') can be an inspiration since the Blues rhythm is the basis of its movement – incidentally, a poem to give great pleasure in group choral work.

Equally within many of our children's experience are the extremes of wet weather and resultant floods. Encouragement for their own work on this can come from newspaper accounts, and again the local newspaper office could be asked to turn up its pictures and articles about the last flood in the locality. Novels centering round the topic include:

*Castaway Christmas* by Margaret J. Baker (Methuen).
*Flood Warning* by Paul Berna (Puffin).
*The Tide in the Attic* by Aleid van Rhijn (Methuen).
In *A Severnside Story* by Frederick Grice (OUP), there is a convincing account of flooding in an old town on pages 139–46.
*The Intruder* by John Rowe Townsend (OUP) comes to a climax in chapter 27 in an exciting account of an extremely high tide.
A full and informative non-fiction book on the topic is *Floods* by W. B. Hoyt and W. G. Langbein (Princeton University Press).

### 56   Summer Storm

Though the word tornado is never mentioned there can be few clearer descriptions of one than in this extract, with the experience of foreboding beforehand and the fantastic stories of the aftermath. The passage leads naturally to inquiry into the nature of these phenomena, perhaps culminating in the form of a display with montages, poems, eye-witness reports, sketches, pictures like the one given on page 67.

*Other Sources*

The relevant chapter in
*The Elements Rage* by Frank W. Lane (David & Charles), especially pages
39–41 and page 48. This book is *the* outstanding source book for all
factual material on violent weather, and includes a number of staggering
pictures. The chapter referred to has a series of amazing accounts of
events of the kind told at the end of the Wilder passage.
A simple book on the lines of the above is in 'The Reason Why' Series:
*Storms* by Irving and Ruth Adler (Dennis Dobson), also *Disaster* by
Sheila Tidmarsh (Penguin).

62   'Oh, they're wicked things'

The middle paragraph should ring a bell. Most of us have stories that have
'become true in time': they may even be family ones. For some children
it may be that the writing out of a story that has 'become true' may act as
a release – in this context it can be funny.

The piano of the final paragraph sounds authentic, but then this fisherman
knows how to tell his tall story! Judging from the surrounding stories
hurricanes move easily from the tragic to the ludicrous, but Jack Williams
is less uncertain on this occasion. Many children will like to try to hit the
right tone for the tall story, written or told, generally in the part of some
'character'.
For a good tall story see *Ventures,* pages 64–70.
Further material and ideas for possible work are to be found in Geoffrey
Summerfield's *Topics in English* (Batsford), pages 76–8.

63   The Hurricane

The poster should encourage further investigation of the nature of storm
phenomena, relating as it does to much of the detail given in the account
which follows. Frank Lane's *The Elements Rage* (David & Charles) would
be indispensable in this connection.

65   The Hell of a Hurricane

A recent eye-witness account. The four paragraphs on page 66 make useful
comparison with the Carlos Williams poem on page 69. The personal
authentic ring of this account can stimulate a variety of work. For
instance, children can look into current disaster stories, in newspaper
reports and elsewhere, and find out personal accounts of this kind.
A whole situation can be revealed or invented, written up, documented,
brought alive through drama and tapes. Jack Williams, Martin and Linda
Sage can give some indications of possible character types in such a
process.

For further reading, see *Hurricane* by Andrew Salkey (OUP), a moving
fictional account set in the writer's own West Indian background. A
similarly involving account of a disaster of a different kind is van der
Loeff's novel *Avalanche* (Puffin). Non-fiction includes an exciting story
in Sir Gordon Taylor's *The Sky Beyond* (Penguin), chapter 13, in which
he describes the saving from destruction of a seaplane in a hurricane.

69   **The Forgotten City**

The poem evokes the feeling of stupefaction so often experienced by the victims of natural disasters, and its form reflects the sense of unrelated disorder. Williams's sympathy finally takes the form of wondering why so much distress attracts so little public attention. He raises, thereby, the wider question of how newsworthy human suffering is.

For a discussion of these issues see *Disaster* (Penguin). For most children the experience of the poem will centre probably on the 'drunken looking people with completely/foreign manners' (assisted by the picture) rather than on the social issues: but the latter should not be ruled out.

70   **Earthquake**

Between two ordinary views of a 'flamingo-coloured kite' the extraordinary happening occurs. It is described in great detail as each ordinary object takes on its new extraordinary aspect, and it is convincingly unreal in its strangeness and horror.

Compare Andrew Salkey's *Earthquake* (OUP, a companion volume to the one mentioned above) especially the 'Story of the Great Earthquake of 1907' told on pages 98–107.

72, 73   **Snow, The Coming of the Cold, In the Black Season**

These three poems on cold are rich in evocative powerful imagery. They become progressively more extreme in forcing connections between things not at first seen as alike: for instance, 'beak of frost' in the Roethke poem or the four words 'rough, black, dark, misty' used of winter in the Celtic poem. These poems are compelling enough to make one wish to try to use language with similar power, to search for connections which will demand recognition as being right. Children often make these connections naturally, intuitively, and need the opportunity for this to happen. An instance is these first six lines of a poem written by a twelve-year-old boy:

**Ram's Horn**

It swirls round
like a tornado
reaching for the sky.
Like a whirlpool
swirling to the bottom of the sea,
disappearing into the darkness.

*The Long Winter* by Laura Ingalls Wilder (Puffin) is a fine clear account of an exceptionally cold winter in the mid-west at the end of last century. One particularly arresting incident is that of the effect of extreme cold on the cattle (Lutterworth, 1962 edition, pages 46–50).

In Philip Turner's *The Grange at High Force* (OUP) the chapter called 'The Great Snowstorm' is a good description of conditions in a part of the Pennines at such a time.

75   **To Build a Fire**

Why did he die? Why didn't he realize how cold it was? What made him take the risks? Would he have been right to kill the dog? How long do we go on believing that he will get through? Why is the story so long? Do we believe it all? What do we feel about the man towards the end?

Discussion on this story may, perhaps, centre, through the authentic and carefully built-up detail, on the exercise of the imagination, and on the contrast between that and the animal's true instinct. The extent of the cold here could prompt work on the problems of living in sub-zero conditions. Also on frostbite see *Annapurna* by Maurice Herzog (Cape), especially chapters 13 to 16 where there are harrowing descriptions of the extreme sufferings borne by the climbers in the doctor's attempts to avoid the worst frostbite results. An astonishing account of a man operating on himself for frostbite occurs on pages 126 and 127 of *We Die Alone* by D. Howarth (Collins).

Geoffrey Summerfield gives full references to material on the Antarctic in *Topics in English* (Batsford) on pages 60–62. Since that date a new, comprehensive, finely illustrated book on the subject has been published: *The Antarctic* by H. G. R. King (Blandford Press).

Films on life at sub-zero temperatures include two on the Esquimaux: John Flaherty's *Nanook of the North* and *The Savage Innocents* in which Anthony Quinn and Yoko Tani starred. This latter was taken from the book *Top of the World* (re-titled later as the film) by Hans Ruesch (Corgi).

Another area of work could be on the extent of human endurance in a variety of conditions. How long can survivors from wrecks live adrift in a lifeboat, or hanging on to wreckage? There are many books on the subject: among them:
*Annapurna* by Maurice Herzog (Cape).
*The White Spider* by Heinrich Harrer (Hart-Davis), astonishing and moving accounts of endurance and rescue on the Eiger.
*The Long Walk* by Slavomir Rawicz (Constable), especially chapter 17, 'Snake Meat and Mud', an account of the last part of a crossing of the Gobi Desert.
*The Longest Walk* by Giuseppe Maniscalco (Wingate-Bates); a deserting Italian soldier walks from the North African desert to South Africa.
*Desperate Voyage* by John Caldwell (Gollancz).
*Banner in the Sky* by James Ramsey Ullmann (Peacock) is a novel centering round the endurance of a boy climber.
*No Beat of Drum* by Hester Burton (OUP) has a gripping account of endurance of a storm at sea in a naval vessel of Nelson's day, and the subsequent relief, pages 102–6.
*On the Banks of Plum Creek* by Laura Ingalls Wilder (Puffin), pages 208–13, gives a picture of the way in which a man can, fortunately, come through cold and blizzard alive.
A piece of music which gives expression to the spirit of human endurance against great natural odds is the last movement of *Sinfonia Antarctica* by Vaughan Williams (Decca ACL 291).

Had the man been prepared to trust the dog he might have saved his life. This aspect of the story could be developed by children interested in exploring the relationship between dogs and men. A group could be given a brief to present the subject to the rest of the class, and encouraged to invite experts from outside to assist in this with talks and demonstrations, e.g. a police-dog handler, a trainer of guide-dogs for the blind. (Incidentally, a brief attached note by the teacher on school notepaper is normally sufficient to validate a letter from the children.)

A passage on the most basic of all responses to one's environment, making a home in it. From what appears at first to be a prosaic account, there emerges gradually through the accumulated detail a picture of skill, experience and, above all, imagination, exercised in a process of interaction between the builder and what he is working in.

The passage can invite an inquiry into the way people use their environment in making their homes in it. Experts from outside can be invited: say, the local borough architect, the architect of the school, a local builder, the manager of a local furnishing store. Designs of the perfect home can be made, whole environments planned using cardboard boxes as the model material, and all the problems of utilization of space discussed. Members of the class who come from parts of the world where houses are not planned as in this country can contribute accounts of what they are used to. The topic lends itself to drama, to be used as relevant: it may be the most effective way to imaginative involvement in living as others live, or as others have lived (e.g. the Esquimaux or the Glastonbury Lake-Dwellers). A simple study can be made of the advantages and disadvantages of our being able to transform the environment for our own purposes without having to pay much attention to its particular nature. Evidence of current environmental problems can obviously be used in this connection: and the whole undertaking sharpened and widened if run in conjunction with the geography or environmental-studies staff. On a different tack, but strongly relevant to this theme, is Ronald Duncan's poem:

### The Site

The site: choose a dry site.
Avoid building against a bank.
Leaning a building to a bank may save putting up a wall,
but dampness will seep through,
you'll see your mortar sweat,
you'll be feeding to keep your pig warm,
this way she'll not fatten profitably;
you may get roast out of it, but no bacon.

The size: floor eight foot by eight foot good –
and slope off to a gutter:
pig's urine swells the bean pods: cover from flies.
Height: that is your problem, your comfort,
for it is you who have got to get in and fling the dung out,
at least once a week, this is most important.

Now is the time to be generous:
Throw the straw in, not in one wad, but two, three, four –
The more straw the more dung,
The more dung the more straw, eventually.
Oh, cover the pig, she'll trample it.

As to the door, observe the stable and copy that:
Make it of seasoned wood that won't warp as mine did.
Don't buy a bolt, get a smith to make one –
Strength, not ornament, is necessary.
And that goes for a pig-sty, and poetry.

An interesting follow-up book in relation to the extract is Wilfred Thesiger's *The Marsh Arabs* (Penguin), which has some remarkable photographs of reed buildings of various kinds made by the marsh-dwelling tribes of the Lower Tigris and Euphrates in Southern Iraq, and descriptions of how these buildings are made.

## 96    Lost in the Desert

Perhaps the key phrase in this astonishing story is 'And all this was hostile to me'. The odds are more heavily weighted against the crashed fliers than they are against the unimaginative chechaquo of Jack London's story. Nevertheless they survive. Certainly the exercise of their thought and imagination plays a part in this, though many of their actions are disastrously unsuccessful, and their survival includes an element of good fortune.

But imagination is central to the story, in three ways especially. Firstly, they exercise their imagination on their chances of survival and on ways of making that more likely. Secondly, the author is imaginatively alive to all that surrounds him, the fennecs, the fossil forest, the orange, even to the extent that 'I almost forgot that I was thirsty'. But this awareness spills over into the third area, in which their imagination plays them false, the whole area of mirages and illusions which make their ordeal so terrible.

Since it is on these responses that much of the interest of the story finally depends, understanding of it can be heightened by work done in following through in detail the reactions in each area. In the second one, children enjoy finding out about desert creatures, about how they survive, and using this information to reckon up the chances for human survival. Consider, for example, this quotation from an animal encyclopedia:

Fennecs live in the deserts of North Africa and the Arabian and Sinai peninsulas. . . . Of the fourteen species of carnivore living in the Sahara, the fennec is the only one able to live well away from oases or other water. It seems to be completely independent of the need to drink, but it will drink regularly and frequently if there is water available. . . . Their main way of conserving water is that of avoiding the heat by adopting burrowing and nocturnal habits.

The problem for the human in the desert is that his naturally low temperature allows the heat to flow from the air to his body. Animal skin temperatures are much higher and they can regulate themselves to adapt to varying conditions. A fascinating area of study, in consequence, is of the various ways in which the peoples who live in the desert have adapted their ways of life to suit so inhospitable an environment. Source books are many, and include:
The Lost World of the Kalahari and The Heart of the Hunter by Laurens van der Post (Penguin).
The Marsh Arabs and Arabian Sands by Wilfred Thesiger (Longman).
The Long Walk and The Longest Walk mentioned above.
The Great Deserts by Folco Quilici (Collins), a superbly illustrated factual account of the world's different deserts and of the people who inhabit them.
The drama possibilities of the Saint-Exupéry extract are considerable. The dialogue can be used, or the author's fluctuating monologue could be developed in improvisation on the mirages. Alternatively, in a large acting area the whole experience could be mimed to the pattern of an overall narration, with the plane crash and the rescue functioning as stable elements.

**A Slave Becomes a Runaway**

This passage forms, in a sense, the climax of the book. Here is an account by someone who knows how to take his mind a walk, or allow his mind to take him a walk, in order to keep alive – the ultimate demand of and response to one's surroundings. It may be that the first sentence is the key to Montejo's success: humility before the puzzles of life, willingness to accept without trying to change, skill in adapting – these are qualities that allow of his survival. But they are exercised in no primitive way: he is 'taking on' his environment in order to be free of a 'shameful' life, he denies himself the company of his fellows in order to be rid of the 'plague' of slavery.

So he eats his pork regularly and keeps fit, while believing that 'townsfolk are feeble because they are mad about lard'. He refrains from walking on trees' shadows at night, but always has enough food. With his natural humour, his superstition, his ability to be alone and to be content, he is all of a piece – a complete man. His kind of physical immediate involvement with his surroundings has given him fundamental knowledge and intuitive understanding that the artificiality of our lives may deny us and which only the imagination can replace and sustain.

How can children approach the passage? Its essential quality is, perhaps, variety: and here, more than anywhere, we must leave room for varied responses to the adventures, opinions, superstitions, observations, that crowd Montejo's pages. The nearest that most of us will have come to his life in the forest are the times spent under canvas in more or less sophisticated camping conditions. And perhaps that is a good point to start from. What is different about it? Why do we normally enjoy it so much at first? Do we retain this enjoyment? Are there times when we are afraid? How long could we endure it? Children can act or write or discuss themselves back into these experiences, and from that involvement may move into some contact with the Montejo experience.

Or they can, perhaps, come in through the slave's tormenting desire for freedom. On slavery there is Jackdaw no. 12, *The Slave Trade and its Abolition* (Cape) which has charts, broadsheets and miscellaneous material, with a list of further reading. In Hester Burton's *No Beat of Drum* (OUP) there is a passage (page 95) that describes the barracoons on board ship. And they may, through the earlier passage from *Huckleberry Finn*, have made contact with Jim, another runaway slave.

On supersitition there are some splendid passages in Twain's book, and a whole literature on the subject. As also on natural medicines: see *Plants that Heal* by Millicent E. Selsam (Chatto & Windus) as a beginning. A whole piece of work can be done on English birds in the same way as Montejo describes the birds of the forest. This can be set off by tapes of real bird song, live or from records (as recommended above). The ordinary suburban scene, for instance, with its starlings, sparrows, thrushes. blackbirds and an assortment of other less common varieties, set in motion by housewives, traffic, cats, should provoke its own atmosphere!

**Charles Darwin, Naturalist, Visits a Tropical Forest**

The book from which this extract is taken is lavishly illustrated and might well form the introduction for children to the work of Darwin. While the complicated personality of the great scientist may not be matter for study by children, the relationship between 'objective' observation and intense emotion evidenced in this passage may well give rise to discussion.

For further reading on the tropical forest see, for instance, *The Amazing Amazon* by Willard Price (Heinemann).

### 122 From a Nineteenth-Century Kansas Painter's Notebook

Is it true of most of us that the violent weather and landscapes are the ones that we release in our imaginations? Do we relate in some strange way to these phenomena?

# Reading List

**Non-Fiction**
* more suitable for the teacher

Perception
* *Eye and Brain* by R. L. Gregory (Weidenfeld & Nicolson).
  *The Graphic Work of M. C. Escher* (Oldbourne Press).
* *The Psychology of Perception* by M. D. Vernon (Penguin).

Artists and Seeing
* *The Journals and Papers of Gerard Manley Hopkins* edited by Humphry House (OUP).
  *The World through Blunted Sight* by Patrick Trevor-Roper (Thames & Hudson).
* *Vasarely* by Victor Vasarely (Neuchâtel: Editions du Griffon).
  *Claes Oldenburg* (Tate Exhibition Catalogue, Arts Council of Great Britain).
  *Form in Nature and Life* by Andreas Feininger (Thames & Hudson).

Flight
*Bird Life* by N. Tinbergen (OUP).
*Wings: Insects, Birds, Men* by Blanche Stillson (Gollancz).

Birds of Prey
*The Peregrine* by J. A. Baker (Penguin).
*The Goshawk* by T. H. White (Penguin).
*The Noble Hawks* by U. M. Williams (Chatto & Windus).
*Bird Life* by N. Tinbergen (OUP).

Environment
* *The Environmental Handbook* edited by John Barr (Ballantine Books with Pan).
* *The Environmental Revolution* by Max Nicholson (Hodder & Stoughton).
  Interdependence in Nature Series (Aldus Books):
  *Man's Impact on Nature* by J. A. Lauwerys.
  *Conservation* by Joyce Joffe.
  *Nature's Network* by Keith Reid.
* *The Silent Spring* by Rachel Carson (Penguin).
* *Your Environment*, spring 1971, vol. 2, no. 1, Urban Ecology: 'Birds in Towns'.
  Connexions Series (Penguin):
  *Living Tomorrow* by Nigel Calder.
  *Disaster* by Sheila Tidmarsh.
  *Fit to Live In?* by Kenneth Allsop.

Growing up in Towns
*Where did you go? Out. What did you do? Nothing.*
*What to do by yourself.*
*And another Thing,* all by Robert Paul Smith (The World's Work).
*Grandad with Snails* by Michael Baldwin (Hutchinson).

*The Penny World* by Arthur Bantam (Hutchinson).
*Mrs Beer's House* by Patricia Beer (Macmillan).

Weather
New Visual Geography Series: *The Weather* by W. G. Moore (Hutchinson).
The Reason Why Series: *Storms* by Irving & Ruth Adler (Dennis Dobson).
* *Floods* by W. B. Hoyt and W. G. Langbein (Princeton University Press).
*The Elements Rage* by Frank W. Lane (David & Charles).
* *The Sky Beyond* by Sir Gordon Taylor (Penguin).
*Poetry in the Making*, 'Wind and Weather' by Ted Hughes (Faber).

Endurance and Exploration
*Annapurna* by Maurice Herzog (Cape).
*The White Spider* by Heinrich Harrer (Rupert Hart-Davis).
*The Bombard Story* by Alain Bombard (Penguin).
*The Long Walk* by Slavomir Rawicz (Constable).
*The Longest Walk* by Giuseppe Maniscalco (Wingate-Bates).
*Desperate Voyage* by John Caldwell (Gollancz).
*The Kon-Tiki Expedition* by Thor Heyerdahl (Allen & Unwin).
*The Voyage of Ra* by Thor Heyerdahl (Allen & Unwin).
* *The Antarctic* by H. G. R. King (Blandford Press).
* *The Amazing Amazon* by Willard Price (Heinemann).

Desert Life
* *The Marsh Arabs* by Wilfred Thesiger (Penguin).
* *Arabian Sands* by Wilfred Thesiger (Longman).
* *The Lost World of the Kalahari* and
* *The Heart of the Hunter* by Laurens van der Post (Penguin).
*The Great Deserts* by Folco Quilici (Collins).

English Life and Landscape
* *Akenfield* by Ronald Blythe (Allen Lane The Penguin Press).
* *Winter in England* by Nicholas Wollaston (Hodder & Stoughton).
* *Journey through Britain* by John Hillaby (Constable).

Teaching
* *Film-Making in Schools* by Douglas Lowndes (Batsford).
* *Topics in English* by Geoffrey Summerfield (Batsford).
* *Team Teaching and the Teaching of English* by Anthony Adams (Pergamon).

General
*Forms of Energy*, Natural Science: An Integrated Course for Schools.
Unit G (Pergamon Press).
*Photography and Architecture* by Eric de Maré (Architectural Press).
*Plants that Heal* by Millicent E. Selsam (Chatto & Windus).

**Fiction**
* better read aloud by the teacher, in extract

    Margaret J. Baker, *Castaway Christmas* (Methuen).
    Paul Berna, *Flood Warning* (Puffin).
    Henri Bosco, *The Fox in the Island* (OUP).
    Hester Burton, *No Beat of Drum* (OUP).
    Meindert DeJong, *Hurry Home, Candy* (Lutterworth).
    Elizabeth Enright, *Thimble Summer* (Puffin).
    Penelope Farmer, *The Magic Stone* (Chatto & Windus).
    Jean George, *My Side of the Mountain* (Puffin).
    Frederick Grice, *A Severnside Story* (OUP).
* Barry Hines, *A Kestrel for a Knave* (Penguin).
* Wolf Mankowitz, *A Kid for Two Farthings* (Heinemann).
    Philippa Pearce, *Tom's Midnight Garden* (OUP).
    Gerald Raftery, *Snow-Cloud Stallion* (Puffin).
    Marjorie Kinnon Rawlings, *The Yearling* (Peacock).
* Hans Ruesch, *The Savage Innocents* (Corgi).
    Andrew Salkey, *Earthquake* (OUP).
    Andrew Salkey, *Hurricane* (OUP).
    John Rowe Townsend, *The Intruder* (OUP).
    Philip Turner, *The Grange at High Force* (OUP).
    James Ramsey Ullmann, *Banner in the Sky* (Peacock).
    A. Rutgers van der Loeff, *Avalanche* (Puffin).
    Aleid van Rhijn, *The Tide in the Attic* (Methuen).
* Keith Waterhouse, *There is a Happy Land* (Penguin).
    Laura Ingalls Wilder, *On the Banks of Plum Creek* (Puffin).
    Laura Ingalls Wilder, *The Long Winter* (Puffin).